HIGH
HOPE

Uplifting stories about home, family and faith.

by

Vicki Marsh Kabat

Inspiring Voices®

Inspiring Voices books may be ordered through booksellers or by contacting:

Inspiring Voices
1663 Liberty Drive
Bloomington, IN 47403
www.inspiringvoices.com
1 (866) 697-5313

Cover design by Jeff Kabat. Photo of Easton Kabat.

Family photos unless otherwise noted.

Scriptures taken from the Holy Bible, New International Version®, NIV®. Copyright © 1973, 1978, 1984, 2011 by Biblica, Inc.™ Used by permission of Zondervan. All rights reserved worldwide. www.zondervan.com The "NIV" and "New International Version" are trademarks registered in the United States Patent and Trademark Office by Biblica, Inc.™

ISBN: 978-1-4624-1288-4 (sc)
ISBN: 978-1-4624-1289-1 (e)

Library of Congress Control Number: 2019920557

Print information available on the last page.

Inspiring Voices rev. date: 01/10/2020

Dedicated to my husband Bruce Kabat

Introduction: Taking back decency

There was a time when people were kind to one another. They brought casseroles and baked goods when someone was ill. They chose not to make their point but to listen to yours. They showed grace and good manners around another's misspoken word or awkward social moment. They did not call names or choose to belittle someone else just because they could. Their words and actions were guided by some inner quality of decency and kindness that bespoke gentleness.

Does this sound like the beginning of a fictional work? This isn't a fairytale, and in some parts of the land, you can still find these pockets of good people with kind hearts who choose to further gentleness rather than grandiosity.

Having played on both sides of that fence, I early on began to seek those moments of grace and kindness. Perhaps I needed them, and so they became my touchstones in a life I will always choose to believe is more mystical than mundane, more blessed than blemished. I expect kindness from strangers and certainly from friends and acquaintances, and I am sometimes disappointed by both. People think I'm naive, but if that ever was true of me, at my age, it no longer is: choosing good and better is a choice.

Divisiveness and meanness permeate our society today in uncommon ways. We no longer know nor practice the art of civil discourse, nor do we debate with intelligence and thought. Our ill-chosen words have become harpoons we furiously launch at one another in hopes that even a few will rip through the skin of our "opponent." Especially if the confrontation can be captured on video and posted on social media for all the world to see—and mock.

Politically, we are so polarized that elections are almost moot. Regardless of what party holds the top office, elected officials are paralyzed by their inability to discuss, debate, revisit, negotiate, compromise and lead. We live our political, social, and religious lives as though every thought and image is a social media moment. And if we hurt someone, all the better—we'll go viral!

I need kindness. I need people to treat me with patience and forebearing. I need forgiveness and mercy. I need to apologize and have you accept that apology. I need new beginnings. Don't you?

1

How do we begin to "take back" decency in our society? I think it must be one word, one thought, one action at a time. In this collection of essays, poetry and photos, I have gathered many such moments. They are examples of wisdom and tenderness, a how-to on loving one another. You would think in the 21st century, we would not need to be taught or reminded of such basic good behavior, but it seems we do.

I hope this collection of my writings through the years helps serve that purpose. In each short passage, I hope you catch the glimpses of grace in your own life. And as a whole, I hope they can serve as a primer for living life well and with grace.

Choosing happiness over being right

I hate him! I don't ever want to play with him again! He's not my friend anymore!"

If you're a parent, you've heard those phrases from your indignant child as he or she comes stomping into the house, betrayed by the best friend of a few moments before.

The first time it happens to a parent is distressing. You try to soothe and console. You ask what happened. You wonder why anyone would purposely be mean to your little darling.

You worry about your child's social skills. You question the play group he's been in. You wonder if the Berenstain Bears have a book to cover this situation.

Just as you are planning a reconciliation meeting between the two children plus a discussion with the other child's mother, in waltzes your child and his "frenemy" calling out happily, "We're going to play football, Mom. See you later!"

As I said, the first time the whole scenario baffles you. It doesn't take long, though, before you learn the best approach to your child's flash-fire disputes is a comforting ear, few words and time.

In Harold Kushner's classic book, "How Good Do We Have to Be?," he relates a story of two parents sitting in a park watching their small children play. One boy grabs a toy from the other, who screams, "I hate you! I'm never going to play with you again!" As the parents watch, the two children turn their backs on each other and play independently.

Five minutes later, they're once again sharing their toys and happily playing together.

"How do children do that?" the one parent wonders about the quick reconciliation.

"It's simple," the other parent replies. "They choose happiness over righteousness."

Our children inherently know what we, as adults, have long forgotten. They know that being right by yourself is not nearly as much fun as compromising together.

Every relationship, whether in the schoolyard, the workplace or the home, requires give and take. Ideally, those are balanced so that no one person does all the giving or all the taking. Ideally, too, no

3

one person always thinks he or she is right and the other wrong.

I'm the first to admit I thrill at being right in a situation, perhaps because more often than not, I'm wrong. There's that moment when you want to exclaim, "Aha! See! I'm right! And you're wrong!" It's a hollow victory, though, when it comes at the expense of the relationship. Holding tight to your moral rightness can be cold comfort, and by the time you realize that, you've lost the moral victory anyway.

These days when my kids come storming in venting about their best friend, I just listen. Everybody needs someone to listen without judgment to the really awful, horrible things we think ... and then forget we said them.

Choose happiness. Now let's go play.

I won the battle

I won the battle
and became defeated.
I threw the gauntlet,
drew the line,
stood my ground
with steady gaze,
unblinking.
I tasted victory,
metallic, bitter,
rusting in
my clenched teeth.
I won the battle
and became defeated.

Imagining solutions

We recently received one of those three-dimensional jigsaw puzzles as a gift. You build it up and out, instead of flat on the tabletop. It takes shape and form and depth and becomes a replica of the actual item—ours is the White House.

It's driving me crazy. I'm a simple person and I like things in my life to be simple. Bread should be white, cakes should be chocolate, ice cream should be vanilla. Puzzles should be flat.

Our youngest son, though, is fascinated with this puzzle. He looks at flat pieces and envisions how they will curve to form an erect portico. I look at flat pieces and see flat pieces.

Nevertheless, we have worked well together on this project. I put together the lawn; he put together the building.

All this makes me wonder whether the ability to see more than what exists is an age-related or personality-related phenomenon. How is it so easy for one person to look at pieces of a puzzle and see the potential in them, while all another person sees is pieces?

Is it that children are used to navigating unlimited possibilities? From the time they first begin to crawl, everything before them is a new, unexplored adventure. Everything for them is imagination and possibility. A box becomes a rocket ship. A dresser drawer becomes a space shuttle. A towel becomes Superman's cape.

When does the towel become just a towel again? When does the cardboard box become worthy of nothing more than the garbage heap? When do flat puzzle pieces become just flat puzzle pieces?

It can't be just age-related. It wasn't a child who invented the first telephone or microcomputer chip. It wasn't a child who looked at a nighttime sky and decided it held more than blackness and twinkling stars. These discoveries were made by adults who never stopped asking "Why?"

Is this desire to invent and discover in all of us at birth? If so, what happens to it in those of us who become content with things as they are? Was it one too many people telling us, "It can't be done. You don't need to worry about that"?

My father has told me all my life, "There's no such thing as a stupid question." It may be the best lesson he ever taught me.

If we don't question the obvious, we'll never discover the mysterious, and I'm convinced that it is in the mysterious that we will find ourselves.

Life is an invitation into the unknowable, the unanswerable. Knowledge isn't a product, it's a process.

If we're lucky, it's a process that never ends. If we're lucky, it's flat puzzle pieces that build upward and outward, becoming monuments to the imagination.

Take time to reach out to the children

Dear," my husband said to me one day, "do you know you have mashed potatoes on your butt?"

"Oh well," I answered nonchalantly, "you know how those church dinners can be," reaching behind to wipe the gravied tater remains from the back of my dress.

Actually, the potatoes came from my 2-year-old buddy at church. As I stood talking to someone at the fellowship meal, he had run up and thrown his arms around me with an excited "Bicki!"

I first met this little fellow just hours after he was born. Holding him in my arms that morning, I felt the warmth of his tiny body fill my whole being. We've been buds—now spud buds—ever since.

Some other close friends recently had a baby boy, also. Once again I was there before he was 24 hours old, casserole in hand, to welcome this newest little soul into the world.

His father gently placed him in my arms and I sat mesmerized by his every sleeping facial expression. What might he be dreaming about, we wondered as we watched him. His journey into this world? Certainly reason enough for that scowl. Maybe those happy little purrs were memories of a life he had just left, one in which he was delivered by God's hands into his parents' hands.

Both of these young boys have families gathered around them, showering them with love and attention. They also are blessed by their extended family of faith—those of us at church who will nurture and love them. We will wipe their runny noses and dish up their mashed potatoes from the serving line as readily as we'll wipe away tears on the playground and dish up Bible stories in Sunday school.

A friend once told me about some people who wanted to get more "quality" children in their program. What a travesty! It's a concept I don't understand, and don't want to.

It is true, of course, that not all children are as fortunate as my two little friends. Too many have no loving circle of family, much less friends, from whom to learn how to love themselves and others. But "quality" is inherent in each child, waiting to be recognized, acknowledge and nurtured.

Our own children may be away at college, or grown and married. Perhaps we never had children. Each of us, though, has many chances to reach out to a child. We can volunteer at school, be a Big Brother or Big Sister, help in the church nursery, or teach an arts and crafts class. The opportunities to help a young child know his or her worth are endless.

And maybe, if you're really lucky, you'll come home one day with mashed potatoes on your butt.

Suddenly a child comes into focus

I was on the neighborhood school track the other evening with one of my sons. He was trying to get in shape for an upcoming athletic season. I was just trying to get around the oval a few times.

We started out at the same point, but he soon sprinted ahead of me. Following slowly behind, I watched him. He's grown a lot this summer, a burst that has left him with suddenly long legs and arms.

He's now only an inch or two shorter than I am, a height gap that's quickly disappearing. As he loped along easily, he seemed all grace and agility, golden-skinned and muscled.

Looking at him, I was simply taken aback at the miracle of this child, and as I watched, I revisited memories of his life. A flashback of happy and troubling moments, of triumphs and near-disasters.

This child has never eased into anything—including this world, when he made his debut kicking at the doctor who waited to receive him. And yet, his very enthusiasm and eagerness to live every moment fully has propelled our whole family in new and challenging ways.

These thoughts meshed into an intense focus as I walked around the track. It occurred to me that at no given time am I able to give each of our three sons that same kind of focus. It seems I can only concentrate on one at a time.

Many years ago, a wise father told me, "I try to give each one of my children what he or she needs when he needs it." Only having one small son at the time, I didn't understand the advice. But in the years since, I've thought of his words many times.

Daily life is a whirl of jobs, school, church, practices, hastily prepared meals, grocery shopping and laundry. Sometimes it seems impossible to focus on anything for more than a few moments. Yet in all that hustle and bustle, our children keep growing and changing. Suddenly, they're nearly as tall as we are and racing ahead of us, not only on the school track, but into life itself.

I wish I knew how to focus intensely on each child each moment of each day. I can't. They buzz around me like bees around a hive and all I can hope is that some of what they experience is sweet and filling.

And so, that father's advice now seems profound—to give what is needed in the moment. That's quite a lot, actually. At each new level of growth and maturity, as the boys broke out of old boundaries and discovered new ones, there has been that moment when they stop and turn back to me for one quick hug—their arms clasping my knees, then my waist and finally my neck as they grew.

"I'm changing, I'm growing, I'm going on ... but are you still there for me?" each hug silently asks.

Maybe in the end, that's the parent's most important role. To remain steadfast. To be there. To wave each child on to greater victories and bigger accomplishments.

On the track that day, my son lapped me several times. That's OK. I was his benchmark, his starting point. Only the future will tell where he'll finish.

Front porch resurrection

The front porch, faced with near extinction in recent decades of "modern" house construction, is making a sweeping comeback.

The very generation that grew up in homes with front porches is embracing them again as its members build or buy their own homes. Drive through any new residential development and frequently you will see Victorian-style houses with expansive front and even side porches.

I admit, the front porch holds a special place in my heart. The three-story farm house of my childhood sat upon a hill, and from the porch that spanned the house's front we could sit in the swing and survey our land as far as we could see on three sides.

That porch was wide and deep enough to handle tricycle races with my cousins, games of jacks, picnics on blankets, and the dreams of a little girl gazing up into the summer sky.

The porch had many practical uses as well. My mom, sister and I would gather there in its cool protection with old washtubs filled with peas, string beans or strawberries just gathered from the garden. As we shelled or snapped or husked we talked about everything from 4-H projects to boys to what was for supper.

On really hot summer nights, Dad would drag a cot onto the front porch, hoping to catch a night-time breeze and a little sleep. To a chorus of locusts and crickets, he would fall asleep in the infinitesimal glow of a million stars.

The porch served as a haven for all of us, man and animal alike. After a few rounds of pushing a lawnmower around our big yard, my brother would take a break on the porch. Coming in from one freshly cultivated field and before moving to the next field, Dad would stop a minute for a cold drink on the porch. Hot and flushed from canning vegetables, Mom would step out on the porch to catch a bit of a breeze. Even the dogs knew the best place to flop besides under a bush was on the cool boards of the front porch.

And there was no place better to be than the porch when a summer rain swept in. You could sit out there and smell the rain coming from miles away; feel that first hint of a breeze, first hot,

9

and then surprisingly cool; see the first drops of rain plop into the dust that layered everything.

Then the full force of the storm would hit, sometimes driving us reluctantly inside as winds lashed the rain farther and farther up under the porch's roof.

I got my first kiss on that front porch, painted its swing one adolescent-bored summer, helped Dad repair its steps, and spent lazy Sunday afternoons on it.

Front porches serve a real purpose in American life. They are an open invitation to sit, to talk, to dream, or to do nothing at all—rare luxuries in today's fast-paced life.

It only makes sense to construct such a feature into our homes, which should be designed as havens from everyday pressures. Front porches soothe the soul as surely as they shade the stoop.

I'm still sitting on front porches. My own home has one that spans the length of our house. It's not quite as deep as my childhood front porch, but still deep and wide enough to hold the dreams of a grown woman gazing up into a summer sky.

Taking turns

When our oldest son was 4, I remember listening to one of his bedtime prayers. He thanked God for this and that, asked God to take care of different people, and then he grew silent. I waited. I opened one eye to see if he'd fallen asleep, and then, thinking he just forgot to say Amen, I said it for him. "No, Mommy, I'm not done. It's God's turn to talk to me."

You don't think your children will school you?

I have intercessory prayer usually before or after my centering prayer time. The first is all about words and thoughts; the second is about the opposite—recognizing the thoughts as they float through your mind, but then letting them go. The idea is not to engage the thought, begin to dialogue with it, argue with it, chase it down the bunny warren, and otherwise become emotionally engaged with it. Trust me, this is not easy. Whether it's an item you need to get at the grocery store or the person who offended you at work, you can revert to "monkey mind" in a nanosecond.

Both prayers are important and good, although I often wonder if intercessory prayer is more for us than for God, since God knows our thoughts before we think them.

I was reminded of my son's experience when a friend stopped by the other day to visit. She is in a difficult period in her life, and she is earnestly seeking God's instruction to her. She told me she'd been asking God to do this and to do that, and in my Spirit, my word to her about her praying was "Be still and listen" (I might have said shut up and listen). Because we are good friends and we trust how the Spirit works in each other, she was able to hear this, and felt it was a true word. I also have discovered that if I have a word for someone else, it's usually one I need for myself as well—I'm just blind to it until that insight for the other comes.

"Be still before the Lord and wait patiently for him,"
(Ps. 37:7, NIV).

Daughter I didn't have

Three names are hidden away in my heart. Sometimes I say them aloud, but softly so no one will hear. They are the names I chose each time I was pregnant. Names that, after each birth, I stored away. They are all names for girls.

My husband I have been greatly blessed with three healthy sons. Life without any one of them wold be unimaginable. It's not hard to imagine, though, how a daughter would have fit into our male-dominated household. Pretty darn well, I think.

She would have been a tomboy. Rough and tumble, with scraped knees and tangled hair. I would have had to drag her kicking and screaming into the bathtub each night, scrubbing away her cherished layer of dirt.

She would have worn sweatshirts and blue jeans and hated ribbons and bows. She would have succumbed to a dress only on Sundays and then sat with her elbows planted on widespread knees throughout the sermon to show her defiance.

I see her winding up on the pitcher's mound or breaking away to make a score in soccer. I imagine her going one-on-one with neighborhood kids in driveway basketball and smiling with satisfaction when she drives in for a basket.

She definitely would have been a match for her brothers. They'd have ended up doing more than their share of the chores and still be wondering how it had happened.

She would have had blue eyes that turned steely when she was crossed or very determined. Fair complexioned, dusted with freckles, she'd have long straight hair and bangs always hanging down into her eyes.

She would have led the Earth Day celebration in her school, quickly lecturing anyone who carelessly tossed away an aluminum can or plastic jug. She would have been outraged at reports on the homeless and would have demanded answers to why this was allowed to happen. She would have accepted nothing at face value, yet would have believed in unicorns and pots of gold at the end of rainbows.

Sometimes at night I dream about this daughter. I see her as a tiny baby, just a few weeks old. She looks much like her brothers did at that age—soft, downy peach fuzz covering her head; dark blue eyes that sparkle; a face-splitting smile when I bend over to pick her up.

In my dream, I walk into her room and see her determinedly raising herself up on thin little arms, her heavy head wavering uncertainly above the crib mattress, her eyes focused and intense as she concentrates. Then—plop—her head and chest drop to the mattress, her feet and hands flail in frustration, and once again, she begins slowly pushing herself up.

Time and nature have determined what our family is. I wouldn't change it for anything. Nor do I ever question God's judgment in sending me all sons.

So, I keep my three girl names tucked away. Sometimes, in the dark of night as I drift off to sleep, I wonder. When I get to heaven, will an angel with straight, tangled hair, overlong bangs and scruffy blue jeans come up to me, put her arms around me, and say, "Hi, Mom"?

I hope so.

I am grateful

For the cooing of morning doves, I am grateful.
For the verdant grass fed by spring rains, I am grateful.
For the bossy bluejay harassing the cardinals, I am grateful.
For the sherbet-colored sky in the east, I am grateful.
For the staccato hammering of the woodpecker, I am grateful.

I sit in gratitude.
It fills me.

Doing nothing a fulfilling pastime

On almost any afternoon of any weekday you'll find me sitting someplace waiting for one son or another to finish one practice or another.

I'm not complaining. In fact, it is often the best part of my day. Why? Because I have a legitimate excuse for doing nothing. I am waiting, and that's acceptable.

I could, I guess, bring along a laptop and write the next chapter of my great American novel, or at the least, another of these columns.

I don't, and not just because I don't own a laptop.

I could bring legal pads and write. I could make lists of things I should be doing. I could make grocery lists. I could bring stationery and write to friends and family who haven't received a letter from me since my first son was born.

I could bring last week's magazines that I haven't found time to read or the book on spirituality that my pastor recommended to me. I could wonder why I was the only one in the congregation to whom my pastor recommended the book.

But I don't. I drop off son one, two or three, find a shady or sunny spot (depending on the weather), and sit.

Sometimes I lay down in the grass and stretch.

Ever notice how often babies stretch? Grown-ups never stretch, and those muscle-stretching exercises before bounding into some aerobic frenzy don't count. I mean the slow, lazy, from the tip of your toes to the tip of your fingers stretches. Where you moan and sigh and relax about a zillion muscles all at once.

While I sit, I listen to birds sing. I study the pattern of tree branches against a brilliant blue sky. I follow a cottony cloud puff as it floats across the heavens.

Sometimes I close my eyes. Some might call that meditating. I don't. It doesn't need a label or an Eastern philosophy to substantiate it. It's just "doing nothing."

We need a Do-Nothing Society of America. No offices to hold, no meetings. Sign me up as a charter member. A proud Do-Nothing-er, not to be confused with a Good-for-Nothing-er.

Therein lies the problem. We often think if you do nothing, you're good for nothing. Why do we feel so guilty about being still?

It doesn't have to equate to laziness or sloth, a lack of initiative or imagination. I prefer to think of it as being assertively still.

We're like this massive ant hill, each of us scurrying down our path, carrying our load, alert for obstacles.

Speaking of ants, let's not judge so harshly the grasshopper's approach to life in that famous fable. Perhaps the grasshopper realizes what the ant doesn't: Life is short. Enjoy it while you can.

Granted, single-minded stillness is a challenge for me. When I sit down to relax I try to watch TV, read a book, do a crossword and cross-stitch all at the same time. But I'm getting better, and I do choose to "do nothing" while waiting for my sons.

All too soon they finish their practices and we must go barreling back into our day. With one last deep breath, I am ready.

So, if you see me half asleep in my minivan or lolling under an oak beside a practice field, please don't disturb me. I'm very busy—doing nothing.

How would you explain hope?

Hope is believing that ...
> ...now is not always.
> ...even in the darkest dark, somewhere there is light and it will find you.
> ...feelings are not facts.
> ...steadfast, everyday, unwavering love will always surpass evil.
> ...you are known and treasured and accepted, even if there currently is no evidence of that.
> ...the very best thing you can imagine for yourself is not one iota of what God has planned for you.
> ...there are rainbows far above the lowering banks of clouds.
> ...the next breath, step, word, action, morning will, indeed, come.
> ....despite feeling absolutely alone in the world, the universe still holds you.

"Why are you downcast, O my soul? Why so disturbed within me?
Put your hope in God, for I will yet praise him, my Savior and my God"
(NIV Psalm 42:11).

More than a hug

When you have young children, some of the unholiest moments of the week can be those just before you get to church. By the time everyone's socks and shoes are found, clothes ironed and debates about optional attendance ended, I usually arrive at church ready to curse everything in sight rather than bless it.

That was the case one Sunday several years back. It had been a terrible morning. I lost my patience, screamed at all my dearly beloved and made everything worse. Guilt-ridden, I walked into the church office to ask for a resource I planned to use that morning when I taught the youth about, of all things, patience.

Our co-pastor at the time, a woman who is as intuitive as she is compassionate, took one look at me and said, "You look like you need a hug." At her words, tears began to slide down my cheeks.

Leading me into her office to her wing chair, she said, "I take that back. I think you need more than a hug." She sat down and pulled me into her lap, and held me there like a mother holding her child. And she prayed with me. Gentle words spoken to a gentle, loving God to soothe a ravaged soul.

Sitting there, one grown woman in another grown woman's lap, I felt awkward and a bit ludicrous—for about two seconds. And then, as her arms wrapped around me and her soft words flowed through me, I felt exactly like what I was a that moment, a 40-year-old child, badly in need of a parent's love.

I imagine most of us at one time or another become that little child who needs desperately to climb into a parent's lap and be comforted. The burly construction worker who supervises a crew of 20 men, the high-powered chief executive who manages multimillion-dollar budgets, the mother who spends most of her days holding her own children. Sooner or later, we all hurt, and it hurts so bad that the only comfort we desire is that of a loving parent. Some may never have experienced that from their own parents, but they still yearn for it, knowing it exists ... somewhere.

It's the same love we ache for when we're sick with the flu and would give anything just to feel mother's cool palm against our fevered brow.

It's the same love that, as adults, we hope to find in a spouse. No, maybe it's an even deeper love for which we yearn. A love so tender and encompassing it could only come from the One who created us.

A few days ago, one of my best friends stopped by the house. We visited and laughed about all kinds of things, but suddenly the conversation took a turn. Listening to her, I realized she was hurting deep down inside and didn't know what to do with it.

I reached out my hand to her and said, "You need a hug." Then I pulled her over to where I was sitting and said, "No, you need more than a hug."

I pulled her into my lap and wrapped my arms around her. Holding her gently, I patted her shoulder in rhythm to the rocking of the chair. And she wept.

One of the greatest gifts we can give to each other is unconditional acceptance. Because we are human, perhaps we can only hope to achieve that for brief moments at a time. But there are moments when it is desperately needed and absolutely appropriate.

My friend is a highly capable career woman, efficient, mature, loving and compassionate. But at that moment, she was a 6-year-old little girl in a mean old world that just wasn't fair. She needed someone to comfort the little girl in her.

The week before, I had been that little girl, and she had comforted me. This week, it may be you.

Don't fight that child inside of you. Sometimes you need to cry. Sometimes you need to wail. Sometimes you need to shake your fist and shout, "It's not fair!"

And always, you need someone there ready to hold you close and give you "more than a hug."

Be kind to yourself

Several years ago when I was on a church staff, we had a new pastor and his standard farewell included the admonition "Be kind to yourself." The first time he said it to me, I looked over my shoulder to see who he was addressing.

I'm not very good at being kind to myself. That really wasn't in the family lexicon. "Get over it," maybe, but not kindness to self. Self was supposed to be controlled, managed, repressed, ignored, triumphed over.

So as I learn more about centering prayer, contemplation and all things Thomas Merton, what I hear again and again is encouragement to treat oneself kindly, gently, lovingly. Be as forgiving and non-judgmental toward oneself as most of us are to others, or hopefully, to our children.

How can we spend so much negative energy on self-attack when what God makes available to us every moment is unconditional love and full acceptance? It's the great quandary, isn't it? But we do.

When that pastor first said that, he was speaking a foreign language to my ears. But, you know, I think it's a language I can learn. I want to be as accepting of myself as God is of me. What? Do I think I know myself better than God does?

BE KIND TO YOURSELF

The fabric of our lives

Some friends and I were having coffee when we began talking about sewing and fabric and our mothers. We discovered that, for all of us, the three are inextricably linked.

I've been known to tear up just walking into fabric stores (maybe this is a hormonal thing). Why? Because of the memories I have of following my mother through row after row of fabric bolts, looking through the pattern books with her (wow, like the biggest catalog ever!), and then walking out with a neatly folded piece of material that she would turn into something beautiful to wear. I love fabric. My brother and sister love it. We buy it, whether we ever make anything out of it or not. It's a fabric fetish.

My friends had similar memories—moments of connection with their mothers that have lived with them for decades. One friend even confessed that she "visits" a certain piece of fabric that she has adored for months—just going by to see it, feel it, dream about how she'd use it. Finally, the cloth went on sale and she bought 6 yards of it. She still hasn't made anything from it, but it's not as far for her to go visit.

Mothers passing on skills to their daughters, sharing the process of creating something from nothing, in unhurried blocks of time working together, the joy of that final twirl in front of the mirror. Compare that to a quick trip to the mall.

Sewing is coming back into "vogue" (the pricey patterns, remember?), and I'm so glad. Here is a trio of middle-age women who can attest that it is sew worth it!

Living the oral exam

Taking oral exams in college used to give me nightmares. Just the thought of a professor grilling me with questions about a subject I was supposed to know would throw me into a cold sweat.

I chuckle now to think back on that. Oral exams? Ha! I am rearing three sons. Every moment of every day is an oral exam.

From the time I wake up until I collapse from exhaustion at night, I am bombarded by questions from my kids. It is their way of learning and as parents, we are supposed to be primed for that "teachable moment" when we can impart wisdom and understanding.

After fumbling through the first several hundred "teachable moments," I began to run every time I saw one coming.

Children's questions seem to fall into several broad categories. There are the nature questions:

• "Mommy, are the clouds bigger than the sun?"

• "Mommy, if you jump really high into the sky will you ever come down?"

There are the religious questions:

• "Mommy, when it rains is God crying?"

• "Mommy, if Eve hadn't picked the apple in the Garden of Eden would there never have been bad stuff in the world?"

There are questions about the body:

• "Mommy, are you kind of wet when you're a baby and your mom first lays you?"

• "Mommy, when my legs have goose bumps is my skin scared?"

Then there are the questions that originate from some secret place in a child's mind:

• "Mommy, do you want to be buried in a graveyard or our backyard?"

• "Mommy, when I grow up can I marry you?"

Notice that all these questions begin with "mommy." There's a reason for that. Children always get the other person's attention before proceeding with their question. It might be Daddy or Teacher, but they don't talk until they have your undivided attention.

Once, after giving distracted answers to one of my sons, he climbed onto the kitchen countertop where I was making a cake, grabbed my cheeks in his pudgy little hands, and with his face inches from mine hollered, "MOMMY!" He got my attention. Then he asked his question. It gives me some little pleasure to watch his 3-year-old son now do the same with him.

Also, kids' questions never come when you're ready for them. You can be driving in rush-hour traffic changing lanes, thinking about what you can cook in 10 minutes for supper when your child suddenly asks, "If I'm growing all the time, will I get to be a giant?"

Huh? It's sort of mental whiplash for the unsuspecting parent—and we're always unsuspecting. Find a time when you're ready to take on the world's mysteries and all your child will ask is "What are we having for breakfast?" This I could have handled in rush-hour traffic.

Oh, those were the days all right, when all I had to worry about was expounding on the Industrial Revolution for a stuffy old professor. After all, the only fall-out from giving a wrong answer was my semester grade.

Giving the wrong answer to my children could affect how they view themselves and their world. What's a parent to do?

Don't ask me. I ran out of answers years ago.

Hungry for You

Like a stubborn one-year-old
I sit in my high chair
and bang the plastic tray
with my fists.
You try to spoon me nourishment
but my mouth is firmly shut,
my head turned sideways as far from you as possible.
You wait.
This is my prayer time
during my growth spurt of anger.
Every moment offered up
as a loud, hurt "No!"
Yet, you wipe the strained carrots
from my eyebrows
where I smashed my palms,
you pick up the bowl from the floor
where I threw it,
and you wait.
In your hands a bowl full of all I need.
And so we sit.
One will determined to win,
the other willing to wait.

When did we forget how to play?

I spent much of a recent weekend playing. That's right, just playing. I can't remember when I have laughed so much. Let me try to describe it for you.

Imagine men and women, boys and girls, different ages, different backgrounds, helping one another make string finger figures. Remember those? A loop of string you wrap around your fingers to make "cup and saucer" or "chicken feet."

Young fingers patiently helped gnarled, arthritic fingers weave the string in the appropriate way. As the figure took shape, young and old laughed with delight and pride at the accomplishment.

Oh but wait! Next came cotton balls! Imagine businessmen and construction workers, psychologists and doctors, professors and third-graders walking around unself-consciously with cotton balls stuck to the ends of their noses with hand lotion.

Pretty silly? You bet! And what fun it was. Unexpected, belly-laughing fun.

When did we forget how to play? Somewhere along the way as we raced to get into the right college and earn the right degree and land the right job so we could marry the right mate and buy the right house, we forgot what makes life right—enjoying it!

I didn't remember how to play alone, sorry to say. I had to go to a workshop sponsored by a local church and facilitated by a "play expert." Where was that job when I was deciding on my college major?

Under the good tutelage of Glenn and Evelyn Bannerman, we sang old camp songs, played a version of hot potato with a nylon ball, and came as close to square dancing as is allowed in church.

Glenn Bannerman is a retired professor of Christian and Outdoor Recreation for the Presbyterian School of Christian Education in Richmond, Va. He and Evelyn travel around the country holding experiential workshops on play and laughter.

As we played, inhibitions dropped like cottonwood leaves in a dry July. People arrived at the workshop with worries and concerns, sadness and complaints, but within 30 minutes, all that could be heard was laughter.

What were the rules? No one could laugh at the expense of another and no on was put on the spot to do something with which he

or she felt uncomfortable.

By the end of the weekend, we rediscovered the child within us. We also discovered that it might well be the best part of us.

When was the last time you rolled down a hill just for the exhilarating experience of watching the world spin around you? When was the last time you skipped rope, played tag, ran through a sprinkler or tried to catch snowflakes on your tongue? How many times each day do you tell your children, "I don't have time to play now, maybe later." Guess what? It's later.

One of the best aspects of play is that there is no right or wrong to it. You cannot fail at play. If you enjoy it, or someone else does, you've succeeded.

And play doesn't cost anything. Silliness isn't on a toy store shelf. Laughter doesn't bubble up out of a cellophane package. Play is an accessible commodity for everyone.

Sounds pretty simple, doesn't it? Not the kind of nonsense we serious adults should be concerned with. Well, stick a cotton ball on your nose and take a good, hard look at yourself in the mirror.

It's never too late to have a great childhood.

There's no reason to be shy about love

Spring and a young man's fancy turns to thoughts of love. Because we have three young men in our household, the subject does come up on occasion.

I've found that things haven't changed much since I was young and discovering the opposite sex. It seems the biggest hurdle still is the first step. Reaching out to another to express interest and attraction is difficult. One misstep and you're plummeting in a chasm of self-doubt and rejection.

Our youngest son may have the best attitude about it, although at his age he has less at stake and more time to recover. He told me recently that he wasn't going to be shy about love. When I asked him what he meant, he said, "I'm going to let them know. I'm not going to keep it to myself."

Oh, if it were only that easy. Bookshelves and movie racks are filled with the stories of people who found it difficult to let others know their true feelings. Offer your heart to another and you are at your most vulnerable, your most exposed. You place yourself completely in the hands of another to accept or reject, and it is a soul-shaking, heart-in-your-throat, sweat-producing moment unlike any other.

Many of us spend our whole lives trying to believe we are worthy of love. Even when we come from loving homes and have supportive parents, there is still that moment when we seek acceptance of our worth outside the network of our family. If we don't receive it then, it can color our perception of ourselves for the rest of our lives.

One such rejection makes it easy to assume our family's opinion of us was counterfeit. When did we ever think our parents knew anything anyway? They must be wrong about this, as well.

On the other hand, if you offer your heart and it's accepted and cherished, it can transform your life. Suddenly you're weightless, floating above treetops, singing with the birds, your spirit soaring into the heavens. You're Gene Kelly singing in the rain! Anything is possible, any task accomplishable, any problem solvable. Nothing can stop you!

Is it possible, I wonder, for that incredible feeling to be tied into something other than another person's acceptance or rejection? None of us wants to be so dependent on others' reactions to us. Ideally, we would learn to love ourselves regardless of whether others do.

Learning to love ourselves and to share that love with others is a lifelong process. It begins with our parents' loving touch the moment we are born. There are lots of mountaintop and valley experiences along the way. Often it seems we take two steps forward and one step back, inching along at a painstaking pace.

The fortunate among us keep moving forward along the path. We come to acknowledge we are persons of worth and value, of talents and skills, of insight and wisdom. To be able to share the wonderful person you are with another, recognizing his or her equal value, is a God-given slice of heaven on earth.

It begins with that first step. Don't be shy about love. Let that special person in your life know. Don't keep it to yourself.

Coping with first-grade freedom

My youngest child just entered first grade.

Oh, how I have longed for this day. From the moment I had my first child, and through each successive birth, I kept one goal in mind: the day the youngest started school full time.

Visions of freedom have danced in my head lo these many years. I could go to the grocery store without children pleading for toys or candy or sodas. I could go into department stores and not have to chase toddlers from the middle of circular clothes racks.

I could go to the mall and not have to spend 40 minutes in the pet store. I could jump into the car without spending 30 minutes buckling belts and straps to car seats.

Oh, and the things I would accomplish in this newly childless state. I would clean, sort and organize all closets and cabinets. I would finish my grandmother's quilt. I would plan meals and buy food a month at a time.

Believe me, I had planned for that first day of freedom. What I didn't plan for was how I would feel as I left my baby sitting at his new desk still wearing his backpack and clutching his lunchbox.

The night before, we thought we had been so ready. The new school clothes he had selected were neatly laid out. His bath had been taken. His lunch was made and in the refrigerator. His backpack was packed with his supplies carefully labeled with his name.

As we laid together in his bed, we had talked about what the next day would bring. We talked about the friends he knew that would be in his class, and thought about the new friends he would make. We talked about his teacher and agreed she probably would have a really nice smile. We talked about lunch, recess and playing on the playground.

"School is going to be so much fun," I said to him confidently.

"Yeah, I guess," he answered softly.

"What's the matter?" I asked.

"I don't want to go to school," he mumbled into the stuffed bunny he held tightly.

"Why? You've been so excited about being a first-grader."

He looked up at me with those big, velvety brown eyes and said, "I'm going to miss you, Mommy."

He fell to sleep soon after I reassured him, but it was a long night for me. I relived his birth, his first step, his toothless grin, his chubby arms wrapping around my neck.

But, morning dawned anew and enthusiasm with it. Off we went to school, confident once again that first grade would be great. He walked bravely into his class, found the brightly colored paper apple with his name on it and waved happily to friends. With only the slightest hug (so I wouldn't embarrass him), I slipped out of the room and he slipped out of my life.

Now it was my turn to be brave. I came back to the house and watched my husband get ready for work. I straightened the place-mats on the kitchen table. Then I straightened them again. My husband walked through.

"You look lost. Are you going to be OK?"

"Just tell me one thing," I said. "If first grade is this hard, how am I ever going to survive college?"

"But this is the day you've waited for all these years. You're free. You have the next seven hours to yourself," he reminded me.

I've decided this kind of freedom I can do without.

Every person has a life story to tell

A few years ago, a member of our church died. I knew him casually and had occasional opportunities to visit with him. In the years I knew him, we never exchanged anything more than idle pleasantries.

When I read his obituary, I was stunned by the extent of his civic and community service. This was a man who had made a deep and significant difference in his world. Yet, in all our times together, I had never once asked him about his life's work. Reading about it in the paper, I felt acutely cheated, and regretful.

A few blocks from us lives a widow whose yard my sons mow. As I was helping my son unload the mower at her place recently, she came out to visit with me.

"Come, come inside," she urged me in a thick accent. She took me into her home and shared portions of her life with me. She was a war bride from Russia who, decades ago, had come to Texas with her new husband. She speaks six languages, but "My English, it's not so good," she laughs. Her husband died a couple of years ago from a stroke. Her daughter lives far away, and she doesn't get to see her often, though she calls regularly.

She lives only a few blocks away, but she comes from another world and another time. Her life is full of fascinating stories about the war and her romance, her life here in America and her family's life. But the outside of her typical suburban house that I drive by every day gives no hint of what lies within.

The other day I shared a meal with a good friend. She and I have worked on many committees together, dished up chili side by side at church dinners, shared stories with each other about our children. Yet that day, she told me that in college she majored in animal behavior and had received a grant years ago to study whales off the coast of Connecticut. As she told stories about going out on the boats to observe humpback whales and belugas, I was amazed.

She now works as a teacher in a totally unrelated field. Looking at the slight figure of my good friend, I wouldn't ever have imagined her on the deck of a boat riding the waves of the Atlantic Ocean in search of whales.

Three people, each of them a part of my life, and each with a meaningful and fascinating story to tell. I spent several years of my young adulthood working as a newspaper reporter. It was my job to find out about the lives of people I didn't know.

I once had a college assignment where the journalism professor grabbed up the city phone book and went down every three names, assigning each student to do a feature story on a randomly chosen person. "Come back with a story," he ordered. "No excuses."

It was a good lesson, one I'd obviously forgotten over the years. Every person has a story. Every life has significance and meaning. A rich history exists all around us, as close as the man sitting next to us at a church supper, as close as the woman down the street, as close as our own best friend. And to dip into that rich pool of experience, all we have to do is ask.

"Tell me. Tell me about your life."

On being aware

I went looking for God today
and saw her land as a cardinal—
a breathtaking red—
outside the window of a room
where I sat listening
to a wise woman tell us
that all of nature
shimmered with the creative energy of God.

Later a big orange butterfly
careened crazily toward me
as though inebriated by the sun—
so flirty was he,
I laughed
at his audacity.

Above the butterfly,
I saw a low-flying hawk
float above treetops—
sure and steady and purposeful—
and I admired his
confident knowing.

Just above my head
on a branch stripped of leaves
and prickly besides,
I spotted the tiniest of nests—
no bigger than my fist—
but snuggly affixed to its fragile perch.
My, how I'd like to meet
the little guy who crafted such a fine house.
modest though it is.

As I walked along the lane,
showers of red and yellow leaves
fell 'round me
and I marveled
that I could walk through leaf-fall
as though God was showering my
bridal aisle, calling out
"Congratulations! Congratulations!
How I delight in you,
Daughter of my heart!"

I went looking for God today
and, just between you and me,
I think God is a little giddy these days.
Even the rustling of dry leaves
beneath my feet
sounds like the divine giggling
of a Creator God
in the deliriums of joy.

Communion

Communion cup
of wine
a small, cheap vessel
holding the
blood of Christ.
Upon its liquid surface
a flame dances
movement and light
captured in
ephemeral darkness
a reflection
from above.
I swallow both,
the darkness and the light,
the liquid and the flame.

My brother

Someone I used to know came to visit me a while back. At one time, we had been close. It had been such a long time, though, since I had seen him.

When I knew him, he was strong, with golden brown hair and kind, brown eyes. His arms and shoulders were muscled from hard physical labor. And his hands—I remember thinking he could do anything with those hands.

They had strummed a Sears Roebuck catalog guitar years ago to soothe me to sleep when I had been stung 12 times by bumblebees. His hands had fashioned elaborate wooden playhouses down by the creek. I was his obedient little "go-fer" as he nailed and hammered and sawed. His hands created beautiful rock gardens and water fountains in the yard, planting snapdragons and irises, phlox and sweet peas. From the ordinary, I watched him fashion the extraordinary.

His hands twirled me to the tune of Roy Orbison's "Pretty Woman" as we danced to 45s in our socks on the wood floor upstairs.

His hands once swung a log at a raging sow that was chasing me as I carried her babies in a gunnysack to the farrowing house. Trembling with fear, I huddled behind him as he led the way.

Oh, he wasn't perfect by any means. He often was moody and quiet. And sometimes, he was just plain mean. He once removed the climbing ladder from a tree and left me stranded, and screaming, high on a limb.

I mostly remember the good times, though. That's what is great about remembering.

I also remember when he left. It didn't seem momentous at the time, but as the years passed, it would come to be. It was a long time before we realized he had left our lives, seemingly for good.

I danced alone upstairs after that. I watched our houses of wooden sticks rot and fall apart. The rocks in his garden were tossed one by one into a corner. His flowers all died.

I finished high school, went to college, got a job, fell in love, married and had children. Over those years, I saw him only a handful of times. I did not know him then at all.

His life had taken hard turns. He had made difficult, and not always wise, choices. We would touch briefly, uncertainly, but never connect, and then separate again for years at a time.

I thought about him often, nursing my memories of him. He had meant so much to me. But slowly, as a flower without water, the place I kept for him in my heart wilted. I came to believe that I would never really know him again.

Then, eight years after I had last seen him, he called to say he was coming to visit. From 3,000 miles away and for no other reason, he was coming to see me.

It was with mixed emotions that I waited for his arrival. It's hard enough to love and let go; even harder to hope to love again and find you can't.

Early that morning, his car pulled into our driveway. I peeked out the window, a little girl once again. He was really here. Still strong, hair still golden brown, eyes still warm and kind. As I ran to him, his hands—those hands that could do anything—reached out and held me tight, gathering up the joys and erasing the hurt.

And I danced in the arms of the man I thought I might never know again—my brother.

Sister Karen, Michael, myself.

My brother's eulogy

Michael and Buddy

Michael was born on a farm and raised to become a farmer, but his heart and spirit soared to different places. He had the soul of an artist, and he saw beauty and possibility where others did not. He often said, "I feel closest to God when I'm creating," and in that he truly lived out his faith. In his elaborate flower beds and gardens, in the vibrant fabrics he accumulated, in the original designs of his magnificent quilts. He was drawn to color and beauty as naturally as a hummingbird to a feeder—which he probably ALSO made!

As his baby sister, I was often his tag-along, and I thought he could do almost anything. He built a small version of a house down by the creek out of wood scraps and sticks, and I happily fetched and carried to be part of such an exciting enterprise. He looked at a swath of grass by the smokehouse and made an elaborate rock garden with a water feature in that place. He made hay bale mazes up in the barn loft and dug out snow tunnels in the side ditches of the hill where we lived so we could ride our sleds through them.

As my big brother, he was also my hero. One time our city cousins were down for a visit and we all went traipsing through a wooded area on the farm. I was the last in a line of six as we tromped over a hollow, fallen log. Except it wasn't hollow. A great hive of bumblebees, thoroughly annoyed by the time I came across the log, set upon me. I batted at them and screamed but it was Michael who came running back, swooped me up and got me out of there. Later, swollen and miserable from about 12 stings, he sat beside me and played a little guitar and sang to me.

I also thought he was fearless. I watched him lead a bull by the ring in its nose, and I saw him scoop up baby pigs into a gunny sack while holding back the enraged sow with a 2 x 4 piece of wood.

I don't know that much about Michael's life in California, where he lived for so many years. But I know he had a full circle of friends and people who cared for him and were blessed by him. In the last couple of weeks, many people wrote to us through Facebook to say how Michael always made them laugh, or gave them wise advice or just was there for them in times of difficulty. He had 30-plus years of sobriety in Alcoholics Anonymous, and he spent many of those years mentoring others. He touched dozens of lives and helped them regain their true selves.

When he moved back to Missouri in 2001 because of health problems, he became house-mate to our sister Karen and her husband David, who graciously provided him home and family. That is when quilting became his passion and his creative outlet. We all three have a thing about fabric—I guess from years of going with mom to fabric stores as children. It was a pastime he shared with Karen and they both created beautiful, original appliqué quilts. He made a wedding quilt for each of his nephews.

He was back here in Marshall for the past 13 years. During that time, he grew close again to his family. He told me once he wanted to spend these years loving mom and dad, and he did. He helped them and my sister through operations and illnesses and through David's death. He gave back in as many ways as he could. I think he understood, perhaps before some of the rest of us, that the only thing in life worth really hanging onto is love. Not grudges or hurt feelings or misunderstandings. Love. And unity. Forgiving each other and getting along. Family is where we usually learn those lessons and it's by no means a perfect laboratory for such hard work, but it's the best we have. And Michael learned to value that, to make amends, and to love—without expectation.

I often didn't understand his choices or his beliefs throughout his life, but in the end, he was just Michael—my brother. My first defender and rescuer in life.

So this is a celebration of Michael's life. A life of beauty and creativity, of sensitivity and forgiveness, of joy and love that he carved out and sustained through some hard times. He was true to himself, to his nature, to his giftedness—and that often is not an easy path. I'm really proud of him for that.

Michael Dru Marsh
November 15, 2014

Waiting for miracles to take wing

There was great excitement when I went to my first-grader's room to pick him up the other day. The class was witnessing a miracle.

Another mom and I were invited into the room and led to a table for a firsthand glimpse of the miracle. As we bent close to see, several small voices cautioned, "Don't bump the table!" We immediately backed off.

Sure enough, hanging fragilely from a gossamer thread was a Monarch butterfly chrysalis, or cocoon. That day, the kids had spotted some orange on the cocoon—a sign the butterfly's wings were emerging.

"Can you see it?" my son asked eagerly. "Get right up here and look. See it now?"

The other mother and I peered intently from several directions but couldn't see any orange. That didn't matter. They saw it.

Pretty amazing stuff. Inspired, my son and I went home to find our own caterpillar to put in an aerated jar and observe. The one we found—minding its own business on a petunia—wasn't a Monarch. It could probably only hope to become an ordinary brown moth. Nevertheless, its journey from one stage to the other would be just as amazing, and when completed, it too would fly.

The next day, I hurried to my son's classroom and asked about the Monarch's progress. I was moments too late as the class had just returned from setting it free. I managed to get a full report from my son, though.

That morning when the kids arrived, a lot of orange was showing and the bright green chrysalis seemed thinner. Just a short while later, the butterfly's head had emerged, its feelers reaching out tentatively. Then, sometime between math and reading, it had come out of the cocoon.

The teacher told me the kids had been wild with excitement when they took it to the school courtyard to release it. As the children gathered around, the teacher carefully opened the cage. The butterfly wavered momentarily at the top of the cage as 19 sets of eyes watched in wonder. Then, it pushed off into the spring sky, managing to flit far enough to make it to a tree where it sat resting, waiting until it was stronger.

Wow. Can any of us grasp how a lowly caterpillar can be transformed into a bejeweled aeronautic masterpiece? How something that begins by inching its way along can find itself soaring into the heavens at speeds of up to 20 miles per hour?

As the kids excitedly told me about the butterfly's release, I realized that even though I had missed the miracle, I was gazing upon another. Nineteen children. Each day of their lives, more and more of their individual colors show through. Here an emerging sense of humor. There a dash of curiosity. Here a surprising display of musicality. There a glimmer of sensitivity.

Each day, their bodies grow and strengthen. It may seem they are not doing much, but their work now is the most important they will ever do—they are preparing.

Sooner than we can imagine, we parents will be standing at a threshold and watching as our children step out into the world. Some will soar immediately, others will climb slowly. Some will grow to become brilliant Monarchs, others ordinary brown moths.

But the journey from one stage to the other will be equally miraculous. And one day, they all will fly.

Where's the gene for accountability?

Some years ago, a song swept the land that told us, "Don't worry, be happy." Today, scientists are telling us happiness isn't a choice. It's hereditary.

I have a plaque on my family room wall that confirms it: "If Mama ain't happy, ain't nobody happy!"

Trying to unlock the secrets of heredity must be like trying to decipher the mind of a teenager—inconclusive, nearly impossible, and sometimes dangerous.

Geneticists use a model some researchers call "one gene, one disorder," or OGOD for short. It's a particularly fitting acronym loosely interpreted to mean, "O GOD, what are they messing with now?"

The theory is that a single gene causes a disease or a disorder. For instance, scientists say they have successfully identified the "bad" DNA for Huntington's disease and cystic fibrosis. Now, some researchers say the OGOD theory can be used to identify traits and behaviors, such as one's propensity to be happy.

In an age when most children's first words are not "Mama" and "Dada," but rather "I didn't do it," I find this gene theory disturbing. It's hard enough getting children to take responsibility for their actions without giving them the ready excuse of bad genes.

If we have a predisposing gene for happiness, we must also have one for anger and depression and greed and stinginess and on and on. Each identifiable gene can become an excuse for our behavior.

"I can't help it if my room is such a mess. I have a messy gene."

"It's not my fault I pushed my brother into the mud. I have an aggressive gene."

"I'm not responsible if I can't eat vegetables. I don't have green genes."

Shirking responsibility for our own actions is nothing new and it certainly isn't limited to children. Look at any trial docket in any court in the nation. You'll find stacks of cases with defendants claiming, "It's not my fault!"

Whether it's "no fault" divorces or "no fault" behavior, it's a faulty premise. Harry Truman, when he was president, had a sign on his desk that read, "The buck stops here." It had nothing to do with his economic policies. His message was clear: I take responsibility for the decisions I make.

How many of us, as parents and citizens, can say the same today? Whether it is how our children behave or how our government behaves, we are a nation too prone to look for others to blame.

I remain doubtful that identifying character genes can be helpful to our society. Unless, of course, the geneticists could find an "accountability" gene. Now that would be a medical breakthrough that could change the world.

Tearing up by the Twix

As I waited in the grocery check-out line I noticed a small boy, about 3 years old, standing in front of me with his mother. Tears filled my eyes at the sight of the nape of his neck. This sort of thing happens to me frequently these days. I am mourning.

Mourning my three little boys who are now men. I long for their dimpled hands wrapped around my neck, their heavy, sweaty heads asleep in the curve of my neck. I long for their round faces and rounder eyes staring up at me incessantly saying, "Mommy! Mommy! Mommy!" I long for the wonder and amazement and joy they discovered a gazillion times a day and shared with me.

How did I not know that wouldn't last forever? It seemed like it would. All this parenting we did to help them become strong, independent, self-sufficient, responsible adults—I mean, really, did we think that was going to work?

It is the ultimate "gotcha" of parenting.

Letting go. Everything we value, we love, we need, we must learn to hold loosely, and be willing to let it run free. I can stitch pillows that read "Stay here and love me forever!" but I cannot live by those words; they are only good for catching tears.

Not enough is written about how to move from mothering to not-mothering. Maybe because no one has really managed it. Maybe because there are no words to express it.

That's why the sight of the innocent curve of a small boy's nape can reduce me to tears right there in the line standing next to the tabloids and the Twix.

39

Art by Vicki Marsh Kabat

Random acts of creativity

There is a terrible tension between our productive selves and our creative selves, but there doesn't have to be. Many of us work in order to have a salary, to support our families, to build security, and what we do 40 or more hours a week may or may not tap into our creativity. If it does, wow, blessed are you! If it doesn't, then we must find space for it somewhere else in our lives.

The Creator calls us to be continuously active in co-creation, and God equipped us for this work. In my fanciful way, I imagine that God installed a customized "playground" in each one of us as a way to escape into a wonderland of awe, imagination, reverence and delight—in other words, to be closest to the image of God in which we were created. And God must wonder why so few of us ever come out to play.

A word from the Kabbalah says: "We receive the light, then we impart it. Thus we repair the world."

We must not ignore what is perhaps the truest part of our essential selves—that aspect created and enlivened by divinity that resides deeply within us and yearns to play with us.

We need it for our individual, holistic health, but perhaps more so, we need it for our corporate health. The world needs repair as never before. That which our society considers inessential (a hobby, a pasttime, an idle pursuit) may in fact be the primary purpose of our being and the key to creation—rejuvenation. And you and you and you hold a piece of the repair kit.

So call yourself, unashamedly, what you most truly are. I am a writer. I am a poet. I am an artist. I am a researcher. I am a composer. I am a ...

At the heart of each statement is I AM.

The messy pile of me

Here I am, Lord.
The pieces of me
swept into a tidy pile
at your feet.
Still a bit of dust
floats in the air.
I made quite a mess, actually.
Sweep me up, Lord.
Make of me what you will.

The music will flow

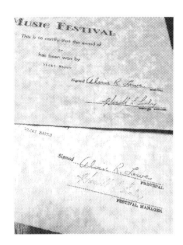

Screech! Squawk! Scratch! What were those horrible sounds emanating from the back of our house? It sounded like a hen house being raided by a fox. Not likely out in the suburbs.

Wait, of course! It was the sound of someone playing the violin, someone who didn't know how.

I was right. Upon investigating, I found our youngest son had pulled out my violin and valiantly was trying to elicit sound, not just noise, from this difficult instrument.

I understood the challenge. I took violin lessons for six years, from junior high through high school, back in my small hometown of Marshall, Mo. It's an agricultural community more comfortable with tractor pulls than symphony concerts. Largely due to the efforts of one man, though, even the farmers of Marshall were exposed to the cultural arts.

That one man was Mr. Harold Lickey, the high school orchestra director and music teacher. Mr. Lickey taught generations of young farm boys and girls to play musical instruments. He taught my mother to play the viola and then, nearly 30 years later, he taught me the violin.

Despite the fact that Mom and I were both tone deaf and couldn't figure out how to count 6/8 time, Mr. Lickey patiently sat with us week after week in our half-hour lessons and slowly transformed sows' ears into silk purses.

Mr. Lickey was a gentleman of the old school. He was thin and small in physique, but when he raised his baton before an orchestra composed of 50 gangly teen-agers, a light came into his bespectacled eyes and he commanded our complete attention and respect. He could whip that baton around like no one we had ever seen, and we didn't doubt for a minute that he meant for us to follow its beat.

Each spring, we had district competition at our school. The orchestra competed, and some of us also competed individually. In my first year to play a solo, I wore a new blue rayon dress covered in lace. It also was my first time to wear pantyhose and low-heeled dress shoes. I was scared to death, not only that my hose would fall down and I'd trip on my new shoes, but also that I would expire from nerves before I had to stand before the judge and play.

Mr. Lickey attended my performance. I motioned to my piano accompanist and off we went, my fingers haltingly covering the neck of the violin and landing, I hoped, somewhere true to the notes I had memorized.

When it was over, I finally breathed and walked toward my seat. Mr. Lickey rose to meet me, took my hand in his, lifted it to his lips and kissed the back of it. Looking at me with one of his radiant smiles, he said, "Well done, Vicki."

The maestro's simple act of kindness and encouragement toward an awkward, scared-silly kid was one of the sweetest gestures I have ever experienced. No one had ever kissed the back of my hand before. No one has since. I was absolutely enthralled.

What Mr. Lickey did for me, he did for others as well in our small town. He led the high school and community symphony orchestras for years.

NBC came to our little burg and did a feature story on him. And Mr. Lickey kept conducting the farmers and grocers and homemakers and their children until the day he died.

Now here stood my son, clutching the neck of my violin in a stranglehold meant only for a baseball bat. "How do you do this, Mom?" he asked.

Memories of Mr. Lickey's inexhaustible patience filled me, and echoing the words he had used with me 30 years before, I gently guided my son's hands along the instrument.

"Here," I said, "place the violin on your shoulder. Your chin rests here. Now move your hand down along the neck and hold the violin gently, like something you love. With this hand, hold the bow. Now, arch your wrist slightly when you play. The music is going to flow from that wrist, and it will be beautiful."

Relax. Rest. Really.

My child,
stop.
Rest.
I appreciate
all your help,
really I do.
But dear,
I don't need it
and I haven't
asked for it.
I'm good at what I do.
You can trust that.
So relax.
Sit.
Breathe.
I've only asked one thing of you,
yet you seek to avoid it
by doing everything—
anything—else.
Love me.
Love me like crazy.
Dance-in-the-rain love me.
Sing-at-the-top-of-your-lungs love me.
Color-me-pictures love me.
But don't work-yourself-to-death love me.

Practicing gratitude

More and more, I am moved to gratitude and humility, but it doesn't come naturally. Talk about faith that moves mountains!

Gratitude sounds like an easy thing to practice, unlike say, humility. How hard can it be to be grateful? I am discovering it often is hard. It's a choice, and one I have to make continuously. Some of us were not born with happy, sunny, optimistic personalities, but while personality is a force to contend with, ultimately it doesn't have to control us.

Our pastor is famous for saying "You can choose what you think." That seemed revelatory to me! For so long, I had let my random thoughts lead me down any old path they chose—and they often chose some pretty ugly byways.

So cultivating a mindset of gratitude can be much like training for a marathon. Many who seek to live worshipfully keep a gratitude journal, or even a simple list. Jotting these down in the evening as you revisit your day is a good way to ease into your training. And if you need to, begin small:

- the carry-out person at the grocer's who took time to really engage me in a conversation
- the way the morning sun oozed into our bedroom and bathed us in light
- food in our pantry
- a cool place to be in intense summer heat
- drinkable water at our fingertips

How much we take these kinds of things for granted!

Now I could choose to live in ingratitude (and I often do, I confess). I could complain about that morning light that woke me. I could resent the carry-out person for wasting my time. I could bemoan the rising cost of the food that is in our pantry. You see what I mean.

God is so good to us—down to the amazing little dots on a ladybug. Surely our choice to complain rather than celebrate must grieve God.

Sign for help

I spent a couple of days recently with our 16-month old grandson, Easton. Each time I see him I'm amazed at the new things he's learned. But this time, I was also stumped.

His mommy has taught him to sign to communicate. I know the signs for "food," "more," "all done," "milk." We have the basics covered—or so I thought.

On this visit, I was playing with Easton while his mom caught a few more zzzz's. We vroomed cars, read books, sang songs, stacked cups. It was a busy day in this little guy's world.

Then he tried to open a lid on a toy but it was stuck. He kept pulling on it but it wouldn't budge. He looked up at me and patted his chest with his palm. What was this? He clearly was signing me, but I didn't know this one. He signed again, his look impatient. So, I gave him a sign—the universal shrug of the shoulders to mean "I don't know." He gave up on me, and that toy, and moved to his blocks.

Later, when I asked his mom what the sign was, she said, "Oh, that's the sign for help."

How brilliant! Talk about communicating a basic need. I wonder how many of us know how, or are willing, to do that? Help, I'm overwhelmed. Help, I'm sad. Help, I don't know what to do. Help. Help me.

Getting past the ugly

There is a show on HGTV called the "Property Brothers." One brother is a Realtor©, the other a contractor. They find less-than-inspiring properties and turn them into the homebuyers' "dream house." As they say to the unconvinced potential buyer, "You just have to see past the ugly."

Today is my 57th birthday. I wrote in my journal this morning: "I am in a better place than I have been in several years. Spiritually, emotionally, physically, I am at peace and I am content. I do less and enjoy it more. I stay in the moment more often than not, and am grateful for that. I let go of many things I used to clutch tightly—whether emotional or material. I find that very little is worth the emotional energy I used to so mindlessly and carelessly invest."

How did I get to this place? It wasn't easy, and it took years. Years and years and some of them filled with the ugly—much of it of my own making, some of it not. I had to learn for myself who I was and who I was not. I had to forgive myself for my own mistakes and quit trying to fix other people's mistakes. I had to forgive others for the mistakes they made that hurt me. I had to take account and ask forgiveness of others. Apologizing has often been my vocation, it seems! I had to learn to say No and learn to say Yes, and knowing when to say which is a life course in itself. I had to learn to be kind to myself so that I could be genuinely kind to others.

My mother kept photo albums of our yearly school pictures. One year when we were at my childhood home for a visit, our youngest son—then about 11—looked through my school photos. As he came to the pictures of me at 11 and 12 and 13, he slowed down and looked closely—at the huge, horn-rimmed glasses, the bad perms, the acne, the bangs cut too short. Finally he looked over at me and, with the greatest sympathy and concern in his voice, said, "Gee Mom, you had some rough years in there, didn't you?"

I did, and they all began long after I left school. We all do. It's called growing up, and with any grace and effort, it's also called growing wiser. Transformation happens. You just have to get past the ugly.

Ally, ally, all in free

Shadows are deceptive. Their shape is changeable. They move as the light moves. Sometimes, when the light is strong, the contrast is sharp and stark; other times, in softer light, the edges soften and blur.

The mystics and our spiritual forefathers and foremothers often referred to our "false self," but it was the pioneering psychoanalyst Sigmund Freud who referred to our "shadow self." It is that part of ourselves that is not true to our essential being, the part we don't want to acknowledge and don't want people to see. Often it is some characteristic to which we are blind.

But this shadow side can serve us extremely well in the first half of our lives. Richard Rohr writes about this so well in his book "Falling Upward: A Spirituality for the Two Halves of Life." As Rohr says, we develop this false self in the normal progression from dependence to independence. It is part of the necessary, developmental step of individuation and self autonomy.

Our sons, when they were moving into and through their teens, tried on different images as often as I wished they'd change their underwear. One day a son might be spouting rap and the next week country and western. One day we're sporting bling and the next, muscle tees or cowboy boots.

I saw my job as parent was to give them freedom to explore these different roles, but also to be their touchstone. At the end of the day, all tired out from pretending to be something they weren't, I was "home," as in "ally, ally, all in free." You're safe here, and I will never forget who you are.

As we enter into the second half of life, though, we should have been doing some serious shadow work along the way. Self-examination, honest appraisal, reflection, prayer. We have much to learn from those in our lives who sometimes have a hard word of truth for us. We won't like it, we'll justify our actions to hell and back, we'll tell our friends and confidantes how mistreated we've been, but all of that is just you and me trying to stay oblivious to those shadows that never seem to want to come out into the light. And they all keep us from being "our best and deepest self," as Rohr says.

What is it that you don't want to see about yourself? What pattern of behavior or communication has haunted your relationships? Is it really always the other person's fault?

I struggle with this constantly, and I think we all do and always will. We don't get there except through hard, daily journeying. Find someone who will love you with accountability, who will love you enough to see the best self within you. Listen to that person. Assess everything with the Spirit as your interpreter. Quit talking, i.e., justifying, and listen. God is "home"—and constantly God's word to us is "Ally, ally, all in free!"

Hot dogs on the altar

I caught a glimpse of myself today in a moment of full concentration. Kind of an out-of-body moment when I saw the way I was sticking my tongue out slightly, left of center, when I'm really focused. The way my hands moved slowly and precisely. The way the noise and activity around me fell away. And what was I doing to invoke this much concentration?

I was cutting up a hot dog for a toddler's lunch at the free lunch ministry where I volunteer. On Thursdays, I'm the chili dog lady, and I do a brisk business at my station, but then the business is brisk at every station. People are hungry, and just trying to make it from one day to the next.

So I'm cutting up this weiner. Slicing it, then slicing it again because I want to make sure no one piece could cause a child to choke. And I am totally involved in this task. You'd think I was a neurosurgeon.

In that instant, nothing was more important to me than preparing for this child—whom I didn't know and didn't meet—food to fill her belly. One less hungry child for at least a few hours. I think that deserves our full attention. I wish a lot more people paid attention.

The Sacrament of the Hot Dog served at the Altar of Need. Amen, and pass the ketchup.

Morning confessions

Confession this morning. I have been, as 19th century theologian Oswald Chambers would say, a "spiritual sluggard." I could blame it on the stifling heat we're experiencing in Texas, or the distraction of ice cream, or the joy of children visiting. Or I could just admit I haven't made spending time with God my all-consuming priority.

I am so lonely and bereft of spirit when I "fall asleep," i.e., do not stay attentive to God's presence in, around and through me. My pastor used a wonderful example of this yesterday, referring to a person who does not know and experience God as a tin man hearing only a hollow echo where his heart should be.

Paul's letter to the church at Galatia hit me hard today. In chapter 5, verses 7 – 8, he writes: *"You were running a good race. Who cut in on you and kept you from obeying the truth? That kind of persuasion does not come from the one who calls you"* (NIV). In verse 6, he sums it up: *"The only thing that counts is faith expressing itself through love."*

Wake up, self! See and feel and taste the goodness of God. Let your heart swell with gratitude. The time for sleeping is past. Now, now, now is the moment of worship and thanksgiving—while putting the dirty laundry in the wash, while pouring that second cup of coffee, while brushing your teeth, while chatting with a next door neighbor.

How can I be love and show it forth today? Tell me how your day goes. Let's encourage one another lest someone or some thing cuts in on our good race.

And then the rain came

This past weekend it rained. Almost 6 inches in one day. We had received less than an inch of rain for the previous three months. This was the hottest, driest summer on record in our state. And then the rain came.

Every living thing raised itself up to receive this long-awaited moisture. You could almost see spirits lift, from the smallest plant to humans who stood in grateful awe watching sheets of water fall all around them. Likewise, you could see the plants greening as the moisture and the nitrogen found the parched roots and revived the plants.

This is how I feel during centering prayer. I lift my head up to receive the love of God, who pours it over me abundantly. My spirit, parched by the dailiness of life, lifts and I feel lighter and lighter. Surely I would die without this downpour of grace and mercy, forgiveness and love.

And like a single blade of grass, I am renewed, sparkling with the droplets of divine sustenance. It is, indeed, the greening of my spirit. I soak it all in.

From strength to strength

Psalm 84: *"...blessed are those whose strength is in you, who have set their hearts on pilgrimage. They go from strength to strength..." (5-7, NIV).*

What does it mean for me to be on pilgrimage? How do I move from strength to strength? The dictionary defines pilgrimage as a journey to a sacred place or shrine, as Muslims are commanded to do at least once in their lives in their journey to Mecca. Pilgrimage also is defined as "the course of life on earth."

Do I consider my days on earth a longing for that which is sacred and holy, or am I hurtling down the mountain of space and time gathering only speed and mass? Is my heart so set on the destination that I am blind to the journey?

If my strength is in the Lord, how do I live out moving "from strength to strength?" I have to be IN the Lord, centered there. *"In quiet and rest is your salvation,"* the scriptures tell us. A day without prayer is a day full of care. Okay, I have no idea where that came from; maybe just another of my cheesy little rhymes, but it holds inherent truth.

We can no more travel each day on our pilgrimage without proper preparation than we could start across the desert without water in our canteen. Yet so many of us hurl ourselves into the day with no more sustenance than a cup of joe and a Pop Tart.

Pilgrimage is a lifetime journey, but the encouragement is that our weakness is made perfect in God's strength, God's strength for the journey.

Wait fiercely

A friend posted this quote on Facebook from Kay Ryan, the former U.S. Poet Laureate: "Who would have guessed it possible that waiting is sustainable, a place with its own harvest."

Of all the things that come unnaturally to us, waiting may be at the top of the list. It is for me. Since I walked away from my job and my profession, my new discipline has become waiting. I had no Plan B when I left, except to love and trust God more deeply, and to wait.

I could spend the rest of my life learning what that first one means. Some days I feel like I'm swimming in a sea of God's mercy and acceptance; other days, I feel beached on a distant shore. But then, so did Jonah, so maybe that's not such a bad place to be either.

Nature abhors a vacuum, and something will rush to fill it. Loneliness seeks company, boredom seeks excitement, pain seeks distraction. So many ideas rush at me to fill this time of waiting. I could do this, or this, or this. Finding something I can do is not the challenge; maybe the challenge is realizing what I cannot do and allowing God to do it through me. Or maybe it is to welcome the void and see what it has to teach me.

I shared with my Facebook friend who posted Ryan's quote how I struggle with waiting, and he said to me, "Wait fiercely, my friend."

Waiting. Waiting upon the Lord. Active waiting. Awareness and gratitude for each moment. Fierce waiting. And the harvest is always now. This. Silos full of Yes!

A living hope

When we run out of grocery money before the next check ...
When the only medication that might help isn't covered by insurance ...

When the scientific data says there's nothing more that can be done ...

When the water bill is twice what we expected ...

When the person we cared about deeply turns his back on our friendship ...

That's when we remember whose we are. Our God carries us just above this furrowed field of facts, then sweeps them away as so many pesky flies, replacing them with fragrant flowers. We are people who do not live by fact but by faith. And we are people of hope.

"In his great mercy he has given us new birth into a living hope through the resurrection of Jesus Christ from the dead"
(1 Peter 1:3, NIV).

Read through verse 9 in this passage. Yes, there are troubles and trials, but our inheritance is being safeguarded. We have a "living" hope, and in that there is no despair. Instead, we are "filled with an inexpressible and glorious joy."

Flies or flowers?

Facts or faith?

The business of God

Sometimes I wish I could go back to believing in something—a creed, a party stance, a dogma. You know, those "things" we create and thus think we own and can control. I could always climb onto these high horses and get my righteous indignation on.

Believing in God is much harder. First, it requires so little of us. Seriously, God has never once asked me to create and submit a strategic plan, or provide measurable outcomes, or even, say, to move my cheese. God doesn't want minutes on our last meeting, or reports on sales contacts I made this week, and God doesn't give annual performance appraisals. God doesn't seem to care about all my great ideas on how we could operate more efficiently and productively or create new markets by branding our product better.

This "following" business is soooo not a business. It's counterproductive, counterintuitive and counter—ME!

So, how do I measure myself, know my value, assess which rung of the ladder I'm on? I'm left sitting alone with no keyboard, iPhone, nothing to "calendarize," and no agenda. Sitting. Alone. Waiting. Listening.

And then a last part—obeying.

Yes, faith is so much harder than action. It asks for none of the skills the world values, and requires none of the outcomes by which the world measures us.

But the benefits, the retirement plan? Much, much better.

Sunshine on a winter's day

New Year's Eve and it's the kind of day that reminds me why we live in Central Texas—70 degrees, a cloudless cerulean sky, warm (but not hot) sunshine, and a lovely, refreshing breeze. It's the kind of weather that compels you to be outside and, perhaps, even to romp and frolic. The kind where it is warmer outside your house than it is in.

I sit on the ground in our backyard pulling weeds. Judging their plentitude, it is a hopeless task, especially since I am pulling them up by their roots, one weed at a time. I wear no gloves or knee pads and am not even sitting on an old bath mat—all sensible and reasonable options. No, I like feeling the dampness of the ground begin to seep into my jeans, the dirt wedging under my fingernails. As I tackle another patch of weeds, my dog stretches out in a particularly lovely expanse of sunshine and sighs contentedly. The warmth of the sun spreads across my shoulders and back, and I soak it in like a snake on a rock. "I'm not sure it gets any better than this," I say to my puppy, who opens one sleepy eye.

There are more efficient ways to rid my yard of these weeds, but this is an exercise of the spirit. It is the middle of winter and I am sitting in sunshine on a day that surely was God's template for every day on Creation Eve.

I am glad for these weeds that beckon me from my kitchen window to come pull them. They invite me into the sunshine and it is good. Very good.

Leave-taking and choices

We had a wonderful weekend. Our son who lives in Seattle was home for a visit, and his two brothers and one of the daughters-in-law were all here. The weather was spring in Central Texas at its best and most beautiful with mild temperatures, blue skies and wildflowers in bloom. We invited friends over, grilled outside, played ping pong, had the music on. It was great!

Then, as happens with visits, everybody left. I haven't quite made peace with that part yet, although it's coming a little easier each time it happens. It's especially hard to see our youngest head back to the far Pacific Northwest because we know it will be quite awhile before we see him again.

I envy friends whose grown children all live within 30 minutes and who think nothing of dropping in or asking for babysitting of the grandchildren. I'd be wonderfully happy to have us all so close. But, jobs and life and personal choices take our children to other places, and because they are independent and happy, we must be happy for them.

So, now we are the parents standing in the driveway waving goodbye to our kids as they drive back into their lives and out of ours. We are the ones who linger until the cars are out of sight, and then turn slowly to enter our too-big, too-quiet house.

Here's the choice we have, and it's the one Jesus sets before us always: life or death. In regard to this past weekend, it's the choice to focus on the joy and laughter, the storytelling and serious sharing that filled our weekend, or to focus on the grief that flares up when they leave. On a broader level, it's our choice to focus on the one bad apple or the barrel of good, the small ache and pain or the 95 percent of our bodies still working well.

Every hour of the day we have this choice. It doesn't mean you deny the grief, the pain, the concern; it does mean that once you acknowledge and make a responsible effort to deal with it, you move on. You look for joy. You appreciate the small thing. You remember God's faithfulness.

It isn't easy a lot of the time, but we are to live and live abundantly. It's all around us if we just choose to see it.

Privacy fences on life

About a year ago, we got new neighbors. A family with young children moved into the house next door that had been home to only one family for more than 30 years. The first thing the new neighbors did was replace the chain-link fence with a six-foot privacy fence. It was a little hard not to take "offence." They hadn't known us that long!

A few days ago, I went to the memorial service for the woman who had lived in that house for so long with her husband and three children. The children grew up and left and had children of their own. The extended family gathered at holidays. Visitors of all ages came regularly to their front door, often for afternoon tea and scones. I was invited to her afternoon table many a time. On summer evenings, you could hear music emanating from their home, piano and vocals, sometimes a lone violin. There always seemed to be music.

Her husband died and then, about three years ago, the woman's confusion and disorientation took her on journeys no one could follow. The grown children came and moved her out of the house into a care facility closer to them. This past week, she died.

It's a familiar story, but the story of her and her husband's lives was anything but ordinary. We were fortunate enough to move next door to extraordinary people more than 20 years ago. We, with our three, noisy, curious little boys. She arrived promptly on our doorstep, moving van still in the driveway, with icebox cookies in hand and a beaming smile. Her husband soon met us on our connecting lawns and, together, we opined about thistles and crabgrass, life and love—in about equal measure and equal ignorance. Too many times to count, we leaned across that backyard fence and shared our stories.

They said at her service that her last coherent words before death were, "Isn't it exciting?" I imagine her coming up to the chain link fence just this side of heaven, leaning across it to kiss the face of a new neighbor, and launching into a little-known song from long ago. "Do you know this one?" she'll ask, and this time, the neighbor will say, "I do" and join her.

I'm so glad there are no privacy fences where she now is.

I carried roses

I carried roses
one year later
to my neighbor's door,
stepping across
our connecting lawns
wet with a nighttime rain,
the shared lawn
we had sighed over
on hot summer days,
wiping sweat from our brows,
leaning heavily on rakes,
despairing greatly over dandelions,
more tenacious than ever we would be.

I walked past
the mulberry tree,
the branches scattering
above my head in rioutous profusion,
that mulberry tree
he had climbed into each fall
and, like Jacob in the desert,
wrestled with as he pruned it, cursed it ...
now unchecked.

I walked past
the mimosa tree
he had planted as a sapling
and carefully mowed around
and watered and supported with stakes,
now abloom with sweet sprays of blossoms.

As I rang his doorbell
I remembered past greetings
the welcoming kiss,
the radiant smile,
the courtly sweep of his arm inviting me in.
I carried roses
one year later
and as the door opened,
I was greeted with a welcoming kiss,
a radiant smile,
a tender embrace
and together, two women
celebrated his life.

Me and my dog

I said to our dog, "Why do you always think something wonderful and exciting is going to happen every time I move? It isn't."

And then I wondered, do I believe that as well? Am I so different from our dog? When an idea dislodges itself from the sofa and walks to the refrigerator for a sack, don't I jump up and follow it, tail wagging? When a dream knocks on the door, don't I race to it, slipping and sliding on the tile to see what lies beyond the door?

And when the idea comes back to the couch with nothing more than a bottole of water ... when the dream reveals only an advertising flyer for lawn service ... don't I, like our dog, drop my head, circle three times, lie down, head on paws, sigh deeply and wait, eyes alert, one ear upright, for the next movement of possibility?

Out pulling weeds—again

When I'm upset or confused or hurt by someone, I pull weeds. I keep a lot of them in my yard for just this purpose. I need them, because I seem to be a personality type that gets hurt easily.

I don't like this about myself. Once I realized it, I have worked hard to be more self-aware and to take positive actions to counteract that initial feeling of being wounded. The majority of the time, the slight or harsh word isn't personal or intentional. So what can I pull up (besides weeds) from within myself to regain perspective?

There are other personality qualities I possess that I can dip into. They're a bit flabby because of underuse, but they're still there and can be pressed into action. I can pull upon confidence, analytical thinking skills, clarity. So while I'm out on my knees (a position I find conducive to prompting humility) pulling up weeds, I first have to brush aside the dead leaves (victim, hurt inner child, withdrawing) to get to the roots of the weed. I have to remember that I am not what I feel; that emotion does not have to rule my action or reaction. It can take me a long time to get all of the root out, and too often, I just pull off the top and can expect that one to reappear.

I pull upon scripture. I cast my cares about all this onto God. "Here, you take this one; she's too ornery for me." I pray to know how to love that person better. I ask that I become more rooted in my own goodness so that when a pesky weed sprouts next to me, it doesn't choke me out. I often just pray, "Help."

And there is always lots of opportunity for me to be out pulling weeds. Someday maybe the lawn, and my spirit, will clear.

Ready or not, here I come!

He came in right before communion, through the back door, hollering out "Hello? Hello?" He was sweated through, his face flushed, and he told everyone right off that he'd been drinking. Our pastor welcomed him anyway, and he sat down next to me.

I tried real hard not to shrink back, because, you know, I didn't recognize him immediately. He just looked like a smelly old drunk to me and God knows, we don't want them in our church.

And he didn't seem to have much respect for our service. He kept mumbling loudly and I wanted to shush him, as I did my sons when they were younger, but honestly, I was a little afraid of him.

Then I listened to what he was saying, I heard him talking to God, praising Him. I listened to him instead of the preacher, who I couldn't hear anymore anyway. He was reverent—in his own way—and he held his open hand up toward heaven and sometimes his words were nearly incomprehensible. Once I thought he might be talking in "tongues" but I think his words were just slurred. I felt pretty sober in my spirit compared to him. And that's when I wondered if maybe this really was Jesus.

I started sharing my church bulletin with him and scooted imperceptibly back into my seat where before I had been listing away from him. I looked him in the eyes a few times and smiled my best accepting smile. I didn't want to be caught totally unawares and acting inhospitable. Still though, I was timid.

He was disruptive, all in all. Made us all uncomfortable, upset our routine, kept hollering "Hoo Yah!" as we prayed, which may have been an earlier Aramaic word for "Amen!" Or a Marine cheer. We kind of politely looked away and silently prayed he'd leave. At one point I looked over at him, and tears were streaming down his weather-worn cheeks.

Yes, I'm pretty sure that was Jesus there the other night, but geez, I wasn't ready for Him to show up like that.

A stiff-necked people

Recently I learned about a condition newborns can have called torticullis. It's a tendency to turn the head only in one direction, sort of a bad stiff neck, if you will. The muscles on one side of the neck are weak and stronger on the other side. If undetected in the early months of life, it can create a flat spot on one side of the baby's head and a permanent tendency to keep the head slightly turned.

The good news is that it's very treatable, sometimes with the help of a physical therapist. The parents must turn the baby's head and stretch and strengthen those neck muscles. Depending on the degree of the stiffness, it can be annoying to the baby or painful. But, it must be done consistently to correct the condition.

It was mind-blowing to me that there is an actual physical corollary to what I have always thought of as a spiritual condition. In Exodus, God is angry with the Israelites because they have become "a stiff-necked people," quick to turn away from God and God's commandments, choosing instead to worship idols. And in Proverbs 29, we hear that *a man who remains stiff-necked after many rebukes will suddenly be destroyed—without remedy"* (NIV). In these verses, "stiff-necked" could be a synonym for stubbornness.

How many ways and times have I stubbornly turned away from God's healing correction? Even though God gently but firmly keeps turning my head to where it should go so I can see more clearly the thing in me that needs to be healed? How quickly do I let my head roll away and back to a more comfortable position?

I have to do the work. Strengthen the weak spiritual muscles and loosen the constraining ones. And depending on what God is turning my head to see, that can be merely annoying or very painful.

It helps me to visualize God as the loving parent hovering over me and persistently moving me ever closer to full health and restoration.

A year not enough time to forget

In one year ...

A baby can learn to flash a smile that melts the hearts of his parents, both sets of grandparents, his aunts and uncles and even grouchy old Mr. Wilson next door.

He can take his first steps, tumbling into expectant, exultant arms.

In one year ...

A 9-month-old, suddenly mobile, can wear the knees out of six pairs of pants, crawling into places a new parent never dreamed she would go.

A 2-year-old can go from diapers to training pants to "big boy" pants.

A 3-year-old can learn hundreds of new words, but none more special than the first time she said "Mama" and "Dada."

In one year ...

A 4-year-old can learn how to kick a ball and chase butterflies, all during the same soccer game.

He can sing all the words to Barney's "I Love You" and the Tiny Toons theme song: "We're tiny, we're toony, we're all a little loony."

In one year ...

A 5-year-old can learn her numbers to 100, the ABCs, colors, shapes and how to recite "The Pledge of Allegiance."

A 6-year-old can learn to play "Mr. Caterpillar" on the piano and perform it in his best (and only) suit at a recital.

She can lose three baby teeth and shine a gap-toothed grin you'll never forget.

In one year ...

A 7-year-old can learn to wobble her bicycle down the street to training wheel-less freedom.

An 8-year-old can slam dunk a basketball 1,000 times.

A 9-year-old can spend countless hours buying, sorting and trading baseball cards with his friends.

In one year ...

A 10-year-old can nail his first base hit and catch his first fly ball for an out in Little League.

An 11-year-old can have her first romantic crush, and her second, and her third.

She can go from lacy socks and Mary Janes to pantyhose and pumps.

In one year...

A 12-year-old boy can grow six inches and change shoe sizes monthly.

A 13-year-old can get braces, acne and growing pains. Not to mention spend roughly 1,327 hours on the phone.

In one year ...

A 14-year-old girl can buy more makeup and hair products than her mother uses in a decade.

A 15-year-old boy can consume dozens of pizzas, 100 gallons of milk, 50 jumbo bags of chips and 20 cases of soda.

A 16-year-old can look ahead and begin to dream about what she will do with the rest of her life.

One year is enough time for a child's life to change in unforgettable ways. But it is not enough time to forget the events set in motion one year ago today.

The siege at Mount Carmel, a compound in Central Texas, changed the lives of all who witnessed it. By its fiery end, 21 children reportedly died. Children who will never lose a first tooth, never ride a first bike, never hit a baseball.

One year is not long enough to understand why those 21 children will never have the chance to grow up.

Note: *I wrote this in 1993, the year of the Mount Carmel seige of a compound outside of Waco owned by the religious sect Branch Davidians. Never could I have imagined then there would be occasion for similar words so many times in the future.*

Defining moments

One of our sons was a freshman in college on Sept. 11, 2001. As we spoke in the wake of that unfathomable morning, I thought to myself that this would be the world event in his life comparable to what the shooting of JFK was in mine.

"This will be the defining moment for your generation," I said to him.

His response came quickly. "We've already had several defining moments," citing the Oklahoma City bombing in 1995 and the Columbine High School massacre in 1999.

He was right. For most of his life, our world has been terrorized by random, more than occasional acts of violence that took not just one or two lives, but the lives of hundreds and thousands. And not in faraway places (which were not far away to the ones who died) but here, in America. When the unthinkable happens, how do you handle that? Do you become hyper-vigilant, or numb? Do you live in fear or choose to be fearless?

Our children have come to adulthood unable to believe in platitudes or easy assurances, or that there is a moral code inherent in all humankind that will ultimately provide security for the masses. Certainly as Americans, they are one of the first generations to come to adulthood in such a constancy of vulnerability.

We have had too many moments that define us, our young people, and now their children. How do we still believe, let alone teach, that, "All will be well," as Julian of Norwich did many centuries ago?

Now, as in every age, all is well only as much as it is well in the individual soul. We can control nothing other than that interior state. But if we can tend it well, perhaps the day will come when we can define our moments, rather than they defining us.

The playgrounds of life

Kindergarten teaches us, among other things, that we don't always get our way. To get along on the playground of life, we can't always be first in line to go down the slide. Sometimes we have to step aside and wait our turn.

This is especially hard when we feel strongly about what we want. "I'll just die if I don't get that part in the play!" "I have to make the team or my life is over!" and the like.

That kind of zeal and drama is to be expected developmentally among preteens and teens, who live with "the end of the world" around every corner.

As we get older and have not gotten our way on many things —first choice of college, a job, a mate, a car, a house—we learn to adapt, be flexible, look for the silver lining. We have learned that we can be bitterly disappointed and survive, maybe even find later that it was a blessing that we did not get what we desperately sought.

Those lessons we learned between our morning snack and afternoon nap are ones many of us need to revisit—especially after every national presidential election. A majority presidency hasn't happened in decades, automatically meaning many in the country are either elated or disheartened.

The challenge is, can we all get back on the playground and remember what we learned in kindergarten: take your turn, share, listen, be kind, remember to ask please and say thank you. Perhaps if we can, some of us will go home at the end of the day with a new friend.

Because folks, America *is* our home and the House and the Senate *are* our playgrounds and recess is over.

We are free

I don't understand. I don't understand violence that seeks to maim and kill as many innocent people as possible. I don't understand the conviction and self-righteousness that drives such action. Whoever you are, you have forgotten that there is divinity within you, that there is divinity within the ones you slaughtered today.

You would have us think there is no safe haven. You would have us live in fear and acquiesce our freedom to you.

Then you also forget who we are. We believe in a man so outrageously in love with us that he sacrificed himself to free us once and forevermore from being enslaved by fear.

So we will ride the subways tomorrow and attend the sports events and go to work and to school and live our lives fully and freely. Because we are so loved, your hatred cannot control us.

And that is something you will never understand.

I really want to learn

I was invited into a civil discourse yesterday about my choice of political candidate for president. I can still hardly believe it! We have all been so fractious, disrespectful, and rigid around this election (2008) that I really had begun to think civil discourse was a dead skill.

This young man asked me why I chose to vote as I did. He said, "I really want to learn."

He is the childhood friend of our youngest son. His family and ours spent many a year on soccer sidelines together, and the boys roamed in and out of our two homes, equally comfortable in each. Now he is married with two precious children, and we keep in touch on Facebook.

From what I know of him and his family, I would guess they are more conservative religiously and politically than I am. Instead of seeing that as a dividing line, this young man chose to try to understand. "I really want to learn."

I don't talk politics with anyone except those whom I know share my affiliations. That's on me, and I'm not proud of it. But it's because when I have attempted to breach those lines, I am so often met with judgment, ridicule and disdain. We've become a nation of rigid, dualistic thinking: "My way or the highway!" I'm right so you are, *ipso facto*, soooo wrong. I am American and if you don't agree with me, you are not! I'm a Christian and if you don't vote as I do you're not —and bound for hell as well! Who knowingly walks into a buzz saw? Not I, said the little red "chicken."

And then comes this FB post: "Why? I really want to learn."

I gave a long, thoughtful response, and in doing so, I articulated for the first time my reasons. For the first time, because no one has ever asked!

I have no need to convince this young man to vote as I do. I just want him to vote. I respect very much the man he has become, and the family who raised him to be so thoughtful and caring and just. I like to think he wanted to know my reasons because he respects me as well—and not just as a nice gesture to the "mom" who fed him all that pizza and those Grandma's Pancakes through the years.

I have new hope this morning! And I am so grateful to this young man for helping me believe that we *can* move beyond this numbing, debilitating partisanship to a nation that really wants to learn from one another.

Order your hazmat gear

Have you ever seen the TLC show "Hoarders"? There are people who hoard in their homes everything imaginable and unimaginable, so that often there is only a narrow pathway, like a cornfield maze, through their house. A team of experts comes in, often in hazmat gear, and carries out tons—yes, tons—of "stuff."

The condition is a mental disorder, and those who suffer with it truly suffer. It would be easy to get all holier-than-thou about this, but it occurs to me that far too many of us suffer similarly—maybe not in collecting material possessions, but in how we hoard things in our minds.

Like the memories of people who hurt us, or the time a neighbor slighted you, or when a friend said something hateful. A boss who embarrassed you in a meeting, or the church friend who told the prayer circle your deepest secret. You can insert your own here. Like the twist ties and plastic grocery sacks a hoarder might hang on to and even cherish, we have our little and big items piled up in our minds. We pull them out and mull them over and feel the rejection and then we stick them back in their place so we can find them the next time.

Just like the TV show, we need a health inspector to come in and declare our minds a hazard to our health, and then hire a team of experts to help us carry the trash out.

I don't know about you, but I've got my own hazmat gear.

Commit to the impossible

Somewhere between being raised by parents and becoming a parent you gain some perspective. My parents are elderly now, and our youngest son is 25. This past weekend, the generations reunited to welcome the next generation represented by our 4-month-old granddaughter Tess. There were a lot of parents in the room that day.

At one point, looking across the room filled with sons and daughters-in-law and cousins, my dad said to me, "Look at what you and Bruce started." I laughed and said, "Look at what you and mom started!"

It begins, doesn't it, when two people commit to the impossible in their wedding vows, and then live that commitment out to the best of their abilities, one day at a time. It begins when they hold a newborn in their arms and look at each other and ask, "What have we done?" And it begins again when the parents load the last packed box and bravely send their now-grown child off to live his own adventures—far, far away from their arms.

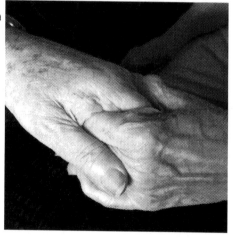

Last Saturday was an emotional day for me. My birth family had come from the Midwest to meet Tess and Kelly, their new granddaughter-in-law. And we all had gathered, too, to wish our youngest son, Brian, the best as he prepares to begin a new life in Seattle next week.

I confess, I don't know how to be this brave, but then, I never have. We aren't. We have this penchant to fling ourselves into the unknown whether it be love or relocation or parenthood. If we waited till we knew how to guarantee the outcomes, we'd never begin.

A surge beneath my feet

After I snaked the garden hose across the yard, I adjusted the sprinkler head just so, and turned on the water. Then I bent to pull some weeds while I watered the grass. And then I pulled some more weeds, and soon I had pulled myself halfway across the yard.

Bent (literally) on that task, I was momentarily surprised when I felt something course under my foot. It was moving and alive and I instantly felt it. The awareness of it stopped my determined weeding immediately. I had stepped on the hose, and what I felt was the water coursing through it.

I laughed at myself and went back to my weeding.

I thought about the sensation of that movement beneath my foot off and on throughout the day, and I realized it was an apt metaphor for how the Holy Spirit desires to course through us—fluid, alive, surprising, unexpected. A movement that stops us cold and pulls us from whatever task we are intent on. A rushing current that says, "Wake up! Here I am! Pay attention!"

But it was even more than that. The feeling of the water beneath my foot delighted me, thrilled me, caught my imagination. I liked it, because it was so alive and powerful and it had connected directly to the sole of my foot and the sensation had shot through my body like a freshet.

Water has long been a symbol for the Spirit, of course. That is no new revelation. But the revelation of how the Spirit can find and surprise us is ever new and thrilling. And I certainly didn't expect a garden hose to be my teacher.

It's not spring yet

The pots by my front door have sat empty all winter. A recent week of sunny, warm days and blue skies sent me to the nursery to buy flowers to fill my pots. When I took my selection of plants to the register, the woman there said, "Thank goodness you've got enough sense to buy pansies. It's not spring yet!"

This morning I wake to a winter rainstorm and a chill temperature in the 40s. No, we definitely are not yet done with winter, even though we long for spring. And nothing we do can make it otherwise.

Seasons must run their course. My brother died in November and it is still very early in my season of grief. When I think of him, he is alive, and then I must remember again that he is not, and sadness swells anew within me. I want to say, "Wait, that's not right." But it is real. Like a harsh winter rain, the pall falls around me.

Suffering, pain, denial, anger—all demand their seasons in our lives. And we must bend to their will. The wisdom teachers of the desert tell us to welcome these hard and bleak seasons. To invite them into our spirits and ask them what lessons they have to teach us. To resist or deny them is only to increase our dis-ease, to multiply our anguish.

By welcoming them—as we might the aunties whose temperaments are sour and bitter and whose breath is rancid—we yield ourselves to a fullness of life we have yet to experience. And we trust that God is in all of it—in the jonquils and tulips when their time comes, but also in the pansies, hearty enough to withstand the cold rain and the gray skies.

Untangling life's problems

Have you ever worked with a skein of yarn? Then you know what happens when you pull the starter thread from the wrong end. You end up with a messy, tangled knot of yarn that would make a Zen master weep.

I'm no Zen master, and I have been working night after night to loosen this tenacious tangle. I am easing this loop through that loop in an effort to get enough yarn loose to knit even one row.

I have considered many options:

1. Throw the whole thing across the room and leave it there.
2. Cut the thread and try to find a new beginning point.
3. Stuff it into the closet where many other half-finished projects reside.
4. See No. 1.

Some nights, I just ignore the twisted, taunting tangle. "Ha, for you!" I say to it, unreasonably. "You cannot get the best of me!" At which point my husband suggests I find a new hobby.

But, I return to it and stoically work with the yarn. I've decided to see this as a spiritual discipline in patience. I become one with the yarn (up to my elbows) and I commune with the yarn (#%{#~^!!). And night after night, I untangle a bit more yarn, knit another row, another length of yarn, another row. It is a long process—far longer than the neck scarf itself.

It's taken me more than five decades to even come close to practicing patience; to learn to welcome whatever knotty tangle enters my life and wait, wait, wait to see what I had to learn from it. This is especially hard for me with hurtful situations in relationships, those sudden, flash-fire emotional explosions that sere everyone within distance. Way too often, I would readily resort to any of the options numbered above: discard the relationship, cut it off and find another friend, stuff it into a hamper full of my other unresolved issues. And yes, even sit with it in petulant self-righteousness.

But if I can ease one loop through another with patience and perseverance, maybe I'll understand the situation better. If I can just keep working with the yarn gently, maybe I'll glimpse another perspective. Maybe if I do that steadfastly for long enough, I'll free just enough grace to carry me a little closer to reconciliation.

Turning off the noise

Maybe an inevitable consequence of so much "noise" in our environment is that we have learned to listen to very little of it. Verbal and visual messages inundate us, and so to maintain some semblance of sanity, we tune out more and more. I understand that, but my fear is that much of that noise is internal, and that we no longer recognize or hear our inate inner wisdom.

Call it what you like—listening to my gut, trusting my instincts, heeding that little nudge—there is within us a frequency transmitting signals. It is an integral equipping that helps us maintain balance, self-protect and innovate. Although I certainly believe the Spirit moves within us and can provide this wisdom, this is also about body and mind awareness—an atunement, a sensitivity, an alertness. Why is my brow suddenly furrowing? Why am I swinging my foot incessantly? Why am I humming? Twiddling my thumbs? Eating this tub of icecream? Needing a drink?

All of these are mind-body connections. If we learn to listen and trust them, they will help us take better care of ourselves. But in order to do that, we first must create space and time to listen to and feel them. That requires stillness, quietude, silence, and there may be nothing many of us dislike more. We have filled our exterior and interior spaces with noise as a barrier to protect us from our own inner wisdom.

We know the answers to the questions we least want to ask, and we need those answers if we hope to experience any freedom, any peace, any genuine contribution to the world. The world needs the answer within us to begin its healing.

Transitions

My husband and I had picked up the 11-year-old girl we mentor and were in the car driving back to our house. Had our car run on words rather than gas, we could have driven to Dallas and back! She had so much to tell us since we had seen her the previous week. She was especially happy about her recent report card, because, as she informed us, "Sixth grade is really scary! They're not fooling around any more."

We could only nod in agreement as she raced on to explain more about transition years: "It's anytime you go into a new school," she said. "Like, I went to sixth grade this year and then when I go to eighth grade, that will be really scary, and then when I go into ninth grade, that will be scary..."

As she paused for a breath, I jumped in: "Or, instead of scary, you could think of it as exciting and challenging!"

"Yeah, I should think of it that way," she said.

With that settled, she was off on a scene-by-scene retelling of a movie she had seen the day before, and Bruce and I were back to nodding and saying "Wow!" at what we hoped were appropriate moments.

The next day, I found some quiet moments and picked up a book I had discovered, Joan Chittister's "The Gift of Years: Growing Old Gracefully," published in 2008. I don't like the idea (or the fact) of growing older. I have not approached it gracefully or with good humor. I am astonished that joints could hurt so much and that energy levels can flag so unexpectedly. To be honest, I find growing older pretty scary. It's like being really engrossed in this great novel with plot after plot unfolding and new, fascinating characters being introduced and then suddenly you realize you know how the story ends. How *your* story ends, and there are far fewer chapters ahead than the ones you've already read. I'm really not looking for a page-turner.

But then I thought about my advice to our little friend. Every transition can seem scary and hard, or we can choose to see it differently. Chittister writes, "One of the gifts of aging is to become comfortable with the self we are."

Yeah, I should think of it that way.

Poor, poor, pitiful me

We have two choices when we are sad and disappointed: to sink into it or to rise above it. Personally, I sink. I admit it. I'm not proud of it. The good news is that when I sink, I stay down for shorter and shorter periods of time.

I find the off switch to my meandering mind and flip it. It *is* true that we can choose what we think about. I find not thinking at all very therapeutic. I put on music. I sing. I recite poetry. Anything to stop the self-pity ponderings.

And I get busy. The best way for me to get over my own sadness is to focus on someone else. I serve food at the free kitchen. I sew blankets for babies in a therapeutic nursery. I visit someone in the hospital. I bake (oh, okay, I don't bake, but I excel at sympathy eating).

I get outside. I walk. I pull weeds. I play with my dog. I dance on the back patio.

I focus on now. This blade of grass. The finch's morning song. The smell of lemon bread baking (at the neighbor's house). The steam coming off my coffee cup. Its warmth in my hands. This breath. And the next.

And I write gratitudes and joys—even when I'm feeling snarky and pouty. There are always many things to be thankful for. There are always moments or people in my day that bless me. I just have to notice them.

None of that changes the circumstance that has made me sad or disappointed. What it has changed is me.

Oswald Chambers writes in a devotion in "My Utmost for His Highest": "The meaning of prayer is that we get hold of God, not of the answer."

I don't always get the answer or the outcome I want, but holding onto God is my choice.

The prickly pruning spiritual practice

When we moved into our home more than 20 years ago, we inherited a century plant right outside our back door. Native to Mexico, it thrives in the Southwest. It has long, razor-edged leaves with thorny tips and for most of its life, that's what you get from it. I guess to survive in a harsh environment it has to develop some sharp, prickly edges.

This morning I realized my century plant looked ragged. There were a lot of dead leaves at its base that needed pruning and leaves from our sycamore had drifted into it and become matted.

I don't love this plant. I would never have gone to a nursery and selected it. But I ended up with it and I feel beholden to care for it.

So, I got my pruning shears and rake and dug down deep and clipped away the dead leaves. Again and again the leaves pricked and cut me, and little drops of blood dotted my arms and hands like a random case of measles. It's just really, really difficult to try to nurture certain plants.

But here's why I do it. Ever so rarely, the century plant, or *agave Americana*, sprouts a stalk or two that can grow as high as 8 feet, and on that stalk, beautiful white blossoms burst forth. It is stunning in its beauty. That's not all. Natives found many uses for this resilient plant—using its fibers to sew leather, its juices (known as honey water) as a sweetener, and its leaves to weave mats.

I suppose most of us aren't much different from the agave. We grow up in harsh environments, and in order to survive, we develop some pretty sharp edges. But hopefully, at least one person comes into our lives—or just gets us with the house—and decides to nurture us. At their own peril and without seeing any change in us for long, long periods of time. It can seem like a century!

But then, when it's least expected, we bloom, and in the core of our being springs a well of sweet "honey water" and suddenly we believe we have all kinds of wonderful gifts to offer, gifts that the world needs.

I have been blessed to have those nurturers in my life. I pray you have as well. And if someone has helped call forth your beauty and giftedness, get out your pruning shears and rake and, oh so patiently and faithfully, do it for another.

Head-over-heels in love

I keep falling in love. Heart-racing, breath-stopping, weak-in-the-knees, I-can't-believe-it's-me love. And each time it happens, I just steep in it, like a teabag in steaming water.

This love transforms everything. I see things I've never seen, hear sounds I hadn't noticed before. There is a lightness in me and a joy. I don't remember the past and I can't imagine a tomorrow any better than this moment. And in this moment, I have everything—and more —I could ever need.

People ask me what my plans are, and I say, "I don't have any." What is there to plan? Everything is complete now.

I don't remember fear, an emotion that ruled my life in so many overt and covert ways. Oh, it keeps trying to get back in, but I laugh at it. I am in love, and fear cannot withstand the power of love.

How many years did I sing "Jesus loves me, this I know," when I did not know? Or I should say I could not accept it. That love is for others, not me. It couldn't be for me. That's the primo stuff; I'll be fine with the consignment-store variety of love.

But then, I heard the love song, I felt the embrace, I breathed in the pure essence of Love. And finally, it lodged itself in my very gut, beneath my rib cage, right dab in the core of me.

I long for my Lover. I cannot get enough of this Love. It fills me to overflowing and still there is more—enough for everyone.

For everyone. For you.

Peeling back the layers

Some workers are in the house this week putting in new flooring. I'm thrilled! After more than 20 years in this house, I am getting rid of the last of the carpet. I am throwing out the can of stain remover. I am going to do a jig on my beautiful new floors!

The workers are also replacing linoleum in the hallway and bath. As I watched one of them rolling up the layers of hall linoleum, I asked him how many layers there were. "Three," he said, "but I've seen as many as five." He stripped it down to the subfloor. "Don't worry. The previous two guys did it wrong, but I'll do it right."

I wonder how many times I've layered over some injustice or wound in my life without first getting to the base of it. When someone comes along and scruffs the heck out of my shiny finish, it's a lot easier to cover it up than it is to try to clean it up. Slap a layer of laminate over that gash and look, I'm good as new. No one can tell.

Lent is a time when we have the opportunity to scrape away those cover-ups, peel back the protective layers we've built up through the years, and expose our hearts. It looks a little battered and raw, that's true, but it's still beating, it still works, and it still has the capacity to love.

Jesus allowed himself to be stripped of everything—his divinity, his power, his following, his clothing, his life. It was complete vulnerability and exposure. They tore him down until there was nothing left but his pure essence, the very reason for his time on earth.

In these days leading up to the remembrance of Good Friday, I pray I can be brave and humble enough to strip away my old patterns and cheap imitation pieties to see what's really there. It may finally be what is truest and best about me.

Breathe in, breathe out

Take any circle of people, get past the pleasantries, and here's what you'll likely find:
—a family estrangement
—a chronic illness
—loss of job or life savings
—domestic abuse
—a family member in rehab
—mental illness
—a divorce
You get the idea.

And probably every person in that circle is feeling not only pain and grief, but shame, isolation, guilt and self-hatred.

It's a heavy load, heavier than anyone can carry. In this Lenten season, can we practice letting go? This has been my prayer in recent weeks:

"Here, God, this is yours. I'm sorry I ever tried to make it mine. I am a broken vessel pieced back together by your mercy and grace. But I find that light pours through my cracks now. I no longer can hold anything but Spirit. Everything else, I put down, trusting that You'll take care of it. Thank you, God."

Feel that? It's your breath returning.

In full retreat

I just returned from a two-day silent retreat. Our church sponsors two such retreats a year, and I think it's a rare gift we can give ourselves of slowing down, meeting God and listening that we greatly need in our society. Nevertheless, it was a rough retreat for me.

When I go into silence, I long to experience epiphanies or even small revelations. I imagine finding the harmonic chord the universe hums and casting my voice into it. I at least want a butterfly to float up and land on my cheek. Right? This is what I paid for.

But none of that happened for me at this retreat. As I sat on a bench along a trail deep in the woods of our retreat site and stared across a canyon, I wept. And I sobbed and I whimpered and I used my flannel shirt tail to sop up my excesses. It wasn't pretty. And no butterfly in its right mind wanted anything to do with me.

It was the start of a silence filled with anger and pain and sorrow. If I had been home, I would have made cookies, knitted a Christmas tree, laid sod. Something, anything to still all those emotions I work so hard to keep locked away. But I had none of those recourses at the retreat.

At the end of the retreat, evaluation forms were passed to participants, and the guest retreat leader later asked me why we did this. "How can you evaluate or rate where and how God has met you in silence?" she asked. "It may have been a hard, unpleasant meeting but one that leads to more wholeness."

She's right. We cannot order up a holy high like we do a Big Mac and fries. Nor is seeking to be in God's presence like watching a sitcom, where plot development and resolution transpire in a pre-scribed period of time and end happily with a flashing LAUGH sign to the audience.

Some people do experience an epiphany and some a wee revelation. Sometimes butterflies or redbirds do appear at the exact instant you have asked God for a sign of her presence. And sometimes, a shower of falling leaves is just dead leaves turning into compost. And sometimes, you go to a silent retreat and you just cry.

When I reread Mary's poignant song, what we call the Magnificat, I remember that this young girl, above all, trusted. She surely had no true idea of what she had just said "Yes!" to, and still she said yes.

She could not have known what lay ahead or how this moment of yielding would lead to the events it did. But still she said yes.

In epiphanies or pity parties, in dancing butterflies or deepest grief, God meets us. It is never in the way we expect, and the only real question is, "Can we open ourselves enough to receive God with our own 'Yes!'"?

Sanctity and spirit

I watch them come
on Sunday morning
old ladies clinging
to one another's arms,
stooped by decades of living,
white-haired and bent,
they come.
Their flowered skirts whipping
around unsteady legs,
their Bibles clutched
to sagging breasts,
stepping carefully in
sensible shoes
to the peals of church bells.

Frail men wrestle
with heavy glass doors,
chivalrous and courteous,
gracious in their greeting.
Friendships of lifetimes
acknowledged
in beauteous smiles
and gentle biddings.

Their eyes cast down,
their movements measured
they enter the sanctuary ...
ritual and rhythm, sanctity and spirit.

Fight, flight or freeze

The human brain has three responses to danger: fight, flight or freeze. An infant really has only one choice: to freeze, or in other words shut down. I have been visiting with a childcare professional who has studied early brain growth development, and her work is fascinating—and heartbreaking.

She is director of a therapeutic nurture center that accepts children from 8 weeks to 4 years of age. Many of the children in this center come from extremely stressful life experiences, such as poverty, illness, frequent relocation, etc. Early childhood is a window of opportunity to improve the neural connections because it is during this time the brain is most receptive, or elastic. It can occur at later ages, but it becomes increasingly difficult to make up those lost opportunities.

When these babies find their environment too chaotic, too stressful, too uncertain, they just shut down, she says. They will turn their head, close their eyes and sleep—their only escape from a reality too overwhelming for them to accept.

I know this feeling exactly. When our oldest son was 4, we went to the hospital with him for what we were told would be a routine hernia repair. Instead, the surgeon came to the surgical anteroom and told us he had found a tumor, and they would need to send our child to a pediatric hospital in a nearby city.

When the doctor returned to the surgical area, I ran to the nearest bathroom and thew up, and then came back to sit with my husband and wait. Instead, I instantly fell asleep. My world had suddenly become too random, too chaotic, too uncontrollable, and, like those traumatized infants, I shut down.

In thinking about this, I began to wonder if the fight, flight or freeze response applies to our faith journeys as well. For those of us who grew up in Protestant churches, we blindly accepted what we were told as young children. Then, in what are developmentally appropriate ways, we begin to question and challenge—"fight," if you will. This is a critical stage in faith development. If one's questioning is met with rigid answers by those who wrongly believe they own the truth, many young believers feel forced to decide: accept what I am being told or leave. Some will choose the first and effectively "freeze" in their faith development. They have learned they will be shamed if they question or labeled as having a weak faith. In a simplistic, dualistic thought process, they will decide that in order to love God they must do and believe as they are told. They shut their eyes and fall asleep to how the Spirit desires to work within them.

Or, they take "flight." The dissonance between their spirit and what they are being taught is too fraught. They can't accept what they often think of as the hypocrisy in the church, so they leave it—and they think they also are leaving God. Again, it's a dualistic approach that results in either/or.

All three responses during our faith journeys separate us from the deep desire God has to be in fellowship with us. To finish this metaphor, let me tell you what my childcare expert said about how they respond to these traumatized babies. They pick them up when they cry, they swaddle them securely in a blanket of love, they sing soft words of love and acceptance to them, they rock them close to their bosom. And they do that, gently and tenderly, every single time the baby cries.

Fight, flight or freeze—or, finally as adults, freedom.

A way out

They say
there's a way out
but to get there
I have to go through
the pain,
the confusion,
the chaos,
the fear.
I have to go through
myself, shedding
layers of lies
like a molting snake.
I can't see very far ahead.
Sometimes the light
goes out completely.
Then I stop
and breathe ...
one - two - three ...
and wait.
They say
there's a way out
but I only have
them to believe.

Pinned by love

Tomorrow is Valentine's Day. I am wearing red and a very special pin.

Several years ago, I was volunteering at our church's free lunch program, where we feed up to 200 people each day we're open. The folks who come through the line are a diverse crowd—mothers or grandparents with toddlers, day laborers, seniors, gang members, the infirm, the hopeless, the determined.

I was serving on the front line, dishing up hot casseroles, salad and bread and handing each heaping plate into hands sometimes too shaky to grip it. Then one of our waiters would come to assist.

On this day, I looked up into the face of a young woman and noticed the pin she was wearing. At first glance, you see it is a heart, but looking more closely, you see the shape is made from the letters GOD.

"I love your pin!" I said to her. "That's such a great design." She said thanks, took her plate and sat down to eat.

It's busy on the frontline. There is always another hand waiting to receive a plate, and I forgot all about the woman and her pin. But then, I heard a soft voice say. "Here, I want you to have this." There she was offering me the pin I had admired. "Oh, I couldn't..." I began, but she stopped me. "I want you to have it."

Looking into her eyes, I knew the giving of this gift was important to her. The only question was, could I be wise enough to receive it?

It is the only question for each of us as God comes in so many ways and offers us unwavering love. Will I receive this love, or will I protest that I simply couldn't?

I reached out my hand for the pin. "Thank you."

We love to give gifts and we would be hurt if they were rejected. Are you rejecting the most important gift of your life?

Receive God's love. Remember to say thank you!

Flights of fancy

A few years ago, based on a movie of the same name, the idea of creating a "bucket list" became popular. What would you still like to do in your life? Travel, start a new business, grow a garden, write a book or a song? The possibilities are endless, of course.

My husband and I don't have a bucket list. I think getting through each day was so all-consuming that it left us no energy to imagine a someday where we would have time, energy and/or finances to indulge in such fantasies. Or maybe we don't have much imagination. Or maybe we were just content in the moment. More honestly, all of the above are true, given any day.

A factor that restricts me from such imaginings is fear. I'm not a risk-taker. I want to get it right the first time. I want to master whatever it is I'm doing—even if that's having fun. I *wish* I were a *bon vivant,* someone who would jet off to Spain just because I'd never been or go bungee jumping or parasailing. I *imagine* I'm that kind of person, but I am not. I don't dive into swimming pools, I ease into them over by the kiddie steps.

That fear not only keeps me from experiencing many new things in life, it keeps me from even trying to do many things. Shall I write that book I have in mind? Start my own crafts company? Go on that mission trip? No, no, better not. The book may not be any good and perhaps no one will want any of the things I make and God knows what could happen on a mission trip. Do you recognize the tape I play in my mind?

I hate it. I really do. It has kept me from so much in life, and now as I am at this mid-stage (or slightly more so) of life, I want even more to jump, to dive, to dig in. Will I? Can I? Yes, I might fail, but I will have learned something in the failing that I had not known before. Or I might appear foolish to my friends, but surely fools have more fun than fuddy-duddies! Or I may risk some hard-earned money in an investment—in me!—that we don't get back. Well, there are so many things that might go wrong, aren't there?

But there are so many things that might go right, too.

In my youth, we lived in a two-story farm house in Missouri. My bedroom was upstairs and a landing separated the two flights of stairs. One day, I stood on that landing looking at the 12 steps down to the main floor and I jumped, believing as I often did at that young age that I could do anything—even fly! And I did fly, a few brief seconds before my forehead crashed into the top of the door that enclosed the stairwell. It knocked me out and I fell in a crumpled heap across the bottom step. I still have the ridge in my hairline to prove it.

My mother was not happy about my flights—of fancy or reality. After it was assured I would live and would not be paralyzed, she scolded me roundly, asking me what in the world had I been thinking to try such a foolish thing.

I can still tell you what I was thinking. That it was possible. That I wouldn't know if I didn't try it. That it might work. That it would be the most wonderful and amazing thing if it *did* work. That's what I was thinking.

And just between you and me, I'm still thinking it.

No, you don't know what I mean

What if I learned how to listen? With my full attention and presence focused on what you are saying. If I could control and reign in my thoughts about self long enough to truly hear you?

It doesn't happen that often. Most of us are terrible listeners. There is an epidemic of self-absorption in the world. Anything we hear or see automatically becomes fodder for self-addiction, not self-awareness. There is a huge difference.

Say you have a problem, you rally the courage to begin to share about that problem with a friend, and immediately the friend says something like, "Oh I know what you mean. Something similar happened to me ..." and thus begins your friend's lengthy retelling of her own experience. That is not listening. That isn't even being present.

Ninety-nine percent of good listening involves not talking. There's a concept!

It also involves not fixing. We can't fix other people's problems. People just need opportunity to give voice to their concerns, to process the situation through talking, or just to release the inner demon for awhile so it becomes less potent.

It's true, we have a lot of "noise" in our world today, and much of it is angry, strident, polarized, dualistic and condemning. These are not voices—they are rants and rhetoric. Probably because when someone first tried to wrestle with a difficult thought and put coherent words to it, there was no one there to listen.

Truly listen. Can you give that gift to someone today?

My wild, bronco thoughts

Whenever I find myself in an emotional slump I go all John Wayne/Thomas Merton on myself. That's probably a pairing you never thought you'd see, but it works for me.

First, I tell myself, "Pilgrim, get off your assets and onto that horse and ride!" And then, I push the bully aside (he got my attention, but I don't have to live with him) and I center—corralling my wild, bronco thoughts—and I contemplate.

The most helpful thing for me to ponder is gratitude, and at the top of the list of things for which I'm grateful is God's tender persistence with me. God never gives up on us. The sweet, soft whisper of the One who created us is a constant refrain underlying the cacophony of our lives: "I love you ... Right now, this moment, I love you ... I'm here ... I delight in you ... Come home..."

I spent decades of my life not accepting those words. Somehow I had convinced myself that my bad was stronger than God's good —geez, how arrogant is that?! But, you know, I believed it in the most shameful, self-deprecatory way—as if that made it acceptable and somehow righteous. And God just kept sending out the sweet invitation.

The God Whisper, gentling a wild and tempestuous temperament, patiently leading us into a circle of love through a narrow gate.

Old men weep

Old men weep.
They stand in gray suits
with rounded shoulders
and remember
wedding nights,
battles fought on foreign fields,
friends lost,
and their ruddy complexions flush
and their spotted hands shake
and they weep.

A lifetime of tears unshed,
of emotions suppressed,
of stoicism embodied.

They are surprised
humiliated really,
these pillars of the nation
who left as 18-year-olds
to fight for ideals and convictions
and returned as old souls at
the ages of 20, 22, 30.
These young men who chain-smoked
in delivery waiting rooms
and stood terrified and amazed when told
they were fathers.
These community and civic leaders
who presided at chambers of commerce
and Rotary clubs, at school boards
and corporate boards.
These fathers who taught
sons to bunt and hit an inside slider
and carried daughters on the tops
of their polished dress shoes
as they danced them around
the front room floor to Glenn Miller.

These middle-aged men
who rode the commuter trains to work each day
newspaper folded crisply under their arm
and rode it home each night—
wrinkled, tired, sagging.

These weekend gardeners and tillers of the soil
who mowed and edged, raked and fertilized,
and went inside to a glass of sweetened iced tea
and a slice of homemade lemon pie.

Humiliated now, that they
would stutter, stammer, falter—
they, who never had.

They are so unprepared
for this unexpected emotion,
these traitorous tears,
this wavering voice.

They look around them
trying to find the person
they had always been—
he, who is no longer there.

So they stand alone
awash in unwelcome memories
an island of loss and grief
buffeted by too many yesterdays
and too few tomorrows,
and they bow their heads
hoping no one notices
that they are old men
who weep.

Looking for meaningful work?

Have you had a mountaintop experience? Those times when God's presence is so real you feel like you could reach out and touch the Divine? When everything—all worries and concerns and fears and sorrows—fall away and you are embodying a "peace that passes all understanding?"

I recently came back from a mountaintop experience—literally, as I returned from a week in the high plains of New Mexico. I was so like Peter at the Transfiguration: "Let me pitch a tent, Lord, and stay here with you forever!" Sounds like a plan to me! Except, there's not much work for a transformed believer on the mountaintop; the work is to be done in the valleys.

Oswald Chambers in "My Utmost for His Highest" writes that when we are brought down from those times of exultation "it is neither beautiful nor poetic nor thrilling ... But it is in the valley that we have to live for the glory of God." (October 2 devotional)

In scrubbing the soup pot after providing a meal for people who are hungry. In embracing the urine-soaked, dirt-caked older man who lives on the streets because the horrors of the war in which he fought make it impossible for him to sleep under a roof. In separating two 2-year-old children hitting each other because in their world if you don't grab it and fight for it, you won't get it.

It is in the valleys of hunger, violence, scarcity and humiliation that the saints must serve. That is where God needs us. Yes, an Omnipotent God who "needs" us—not to bring about the Divine Potential, but to embody fully what it means to love one another.

The air smells much better on the mountaintop but it is our job to bring that sweet essence to the homeless, the hungry, the embittered, the forsaken and the forgotten.

We all want meaningful work to do. Here's the good news: There are many vacancies! Applications are being accepted! No urine test required. Compensation commensurate with your love. Great retirement benefits.

Goodbye, MeMe, see you next time

Goodbye, MeMe," I said, waving to my 82-year-old grandmother as my new husband and I left the home place in Missouri to begin our married life together in Texas. "See you next time!" I promised.

But as we drove south, I swallowed back tears. After all, when one is 82 there are no promises there will be a next time.

More than a year later, we visited home again, this time newly pregnant and eager to share our excitement.

"Goodbye, MeMe," I said, holding her close against my expanded abdomen, breathing in the Avon scent of her I knew so well. "See you next time."

Driving away, I held my stomach and wondered if the baby being nurtured there would ever have the chance to know MeMe. Would he get the chance to cut his teeth on her buttery sugar cookies, as I did? Would he get to fall asleep snuggled against her flannel gown listening to stories of her childhood, as I did? Would he get to stand beneath her cuckoo clock and giggle with glee when the bird came out to call the hour, as I did? And then beg her to stop it at night so he could go to sleep?

Four years later, I scooped up our second infant son from MeMe's lap as we prepared to leave after another visit. "Goodbye, MeMe. See you next time," I said, touching her thinning silvery hair, which she used to tolerantly let me style and curl when I was a young girl.

And driving away, the tears fell silently down my cheeks.

"Don't you know your grandmother will outlive us all?" my husband asked, trying to make me feel better. Maybe she will, I thought. If anyone can, she can.

MeMe had several illnesses in her life—ordinary ones and extraordinary ones. A sleeping sickness in middle age that no one understood or knew how to treat felled her for many months. They thought they'd lose her then, but she came back.

Later she was in a car wreck. Driving home from town, she reached down to retrieve a Christmas present that had slipped from the passenger seat, and she drove into a ditch. She broke her nose that time, but she came back.

More recently, she had a small stroke, stumbling as she walked from her house out to her flowerbeds. She was in the hospital, but she fully recovered, and once again she came back.

On her 100th birthday, we feted MeMe with cake and ice cream, candles and gifts, and bouquets of the beautiful flowers she had always loved.

"Goodbye, MeMe," I said, looking deeply into her twinkling blue eyes to make sure she could see me. "Vicki?" she smiled broadly. "Is that you?" I placed the palm of my hand on her cheek, her skin as smooth and delicate as a rose petal. "It's me, MeMe," I answered. And later, when I said goodbye, I whispered once again, "See you next time."

Even after all these years of saying goodbye, the next time came sooner than I thought it would—just four months later. This time the tears fell softly on the spray of roses on her casket as one last time I looked into the face I loved so much and said, "Goodbye, MeMe. Wait for me. I'll see you next time ..."

Hey lover. Can I call you that?

Recently a former colleague from the academic world in which I worked for several years asked me how I would like to be acknowledged these days. She wants to expand some research we had collaborated on a few years ago and wants to credit my work.

I laughed. Acknowledged? I knew what she was asking. In many spheres, academia high among them, your title and educational rank are extremely important. The more initials after your name the more impressive. The differences among "lecturer," "assistant professor" and "professor" are monumental on a university campus.

But I had stepped away from all of that. I have a bachelor's degree, but no more. I had many professional titles, but no more. I have been a graduate student, but no more. Truthfully, this past year for me has been about trying to become me—my fully authentic, true self. And that self has nothing to do with acknowledgement and egotism. I no longer have a title and by many standards that infers something about my worth. Titles always infer something about worth, and Americans just thrive on them.

We are so uncivil to one another. It goes far beyond political or religious rhetoric. Hatred and intolerance, articulated for any cause, creates the dark, fetid soil in which violent actions take root. Ask

James Holmes, the alleged shooter who walked into a public theatre in Aurora, CO, with weapons designed for mass slaying, and did just that. There have been so many dark instances along our path as a nation.

Frank Bruni, in an op-ed piece for *The New York Times* (July 24, 2012) wrote thoughtfully and intelligently (remember those two words) about labeling and its gratuitous and self-serving abuses. His piece was on Michele Bachmann, a candidate for the Republican nomination for the 2012 national presidency, and her affinity to refer to herself as Christian. He writes that his purpose "isn't to relitigate Bachman's crimes against reason and decency, all widely documented," but "to wonder why we accept her descriptions of herself, and in turn describe her, as a deeply religious woman."

Why indeed? Where is the voice of the "deeply religious" man and woman today? Who is the prophet among us who can still recognize blasphemy and then have the courage to call it out? It isn't a matter of who possesses the truth (God forbid—remember, he did in the Garden of Eden?). It's about where is the humble, discerning, quiet heart that can disengage his or her ego to seek the "still, small voice of God"?

Any thoughtful, intelligent persons seeking to live out the gospel truths—regardless of what label they affiliate with—should be these prophets. Jesus called us sheep and goats (Matthew 25:31-46). The righteous, the "sheep," will be separated to the right and the "goats" —"you who are cursed"—to the left. And what is the basis for this harsh judgment? *"I tell you the truth, whatever you did for one of the least of these brothers of mine, you did for me."*

The litmus test of "the least" include those who are hungry and were given something to eat, those who were thirsty and given something to drink, the stranger among you that you invited in, the ones who needed clothes and you clothed them, the ones in prison you visited.

It would not take a theologian or a political commentator to line up current and proposed federal funding for "the least of these" in our nation to figure out where our contemporary sheep and goats are. Look at food funding, at health insurance, at immigration, just to name a few. Isn't it interesting that the labels we give those groups, the Conservative Right and the Liberal Left, actually line up almost directly *opposite* to Jesus's definition of right and left.

Nor does it allow us to excuse ourselves from action. We cannot lie low as a faithful follower of God and let this become someone else's "thing." We cannot say, "Oh, hunger is just too big of an issue for my contributions to matter." We're talking about the difference one peanut butter and jelly sandwich would make to the homeless man on the corner. In that moment, it's all the difference in the world. You are not being asked to "solve hunger"; you are being asked to feed one person when that person is hungry. What if all we good, Christian folks who so love throwing pot-luck and fellowship dinners and picnics on the ground—all to stuff our overfed selves—cast some of that food out onto the waters of our inner-city streets, our refugee resettlement camps or to the hungry child dumpster-diving in the alley behind your church?

Frederic and Mary Ann Brussat with "Spirituality and Practice" say that, "Labeling is a feeble attempt to control life and create security instead of simply letting what is be." I interpret that to mean that, primarily as fear-based individuals, we believe that if we can name it, draw up rules about it, follow those rules, make sure everyone follows the same rules, then we will be safe. We can control it. According to information about the Enneagram, a spiritual tool to help identify primary personality traits in individuals, half of Americans are in the fear-based sector (Number 6). Wow. Now that's something to fear!

Are you a deeply religious person? Are you also a thoughtful and intelligent person? The two are not synonymous. Are you waiting for others, the many-initialed ones, to speak for you? Why? God's question of what did you do or not do for me will be addressed to you—not just to the learned or the ones who yell loudest. Silent acquiescence was never a ground rule for "accepting Christ." Speak up. Act up.

In Bruni's op-ed dated July 24 he writes: "Bachmann's concept of Christian love brims with hate, and she has a deep satchel of stones to throw. From what kind of messiah did she learn that?"

That is a question for each of us.

How do we regain basic civility? How do we move away from fear mongering? How do we follow Christ? Jean Vanier began the L'Arche movement, residential homes for disabled adults. In his book "Community and Growth," he writes:

"Each human being, however small or weak, has something to bring to humanity. As we start to really get to know others, as we begin to listen to each other's stories, things begin to change. We begin the movement from exclusion to inclusion, from fear to trust, from closeness to openness, from judgment and prejudice to forgiveness and understanding. It is a movement of the heart."

Shall I give you a label? A group to belong to? A title that conveys worth and value? I will.

Lover.

One who loves self as created in God's image.

One who loves others.

One who loves every time, in every situation.

One who loves without expectation.

Heal our brokenness

Oh Lord,
heal our broken world.
Heal the brokenness that would cause someone
to no longer value life.
Heal the brokenness in the heart whose religion
has become hate instead of love.
Heal the brokenness of economic, education and health systems
that no longer seek to help all equally.
Heal the brokenness in my heart that causes me
to lash out instead of lean in.

Lord, we confess that we broke your beautiful world.
We proclaim that you sent your son to heal and free us.
Revive in us this reality
so that we can stand firm in it
rather than be engulfed by so much
brokenness.

Nothing I need now

My faithful companion,
my patient teacher
and loving parent.
Never did You forsake me
and even through great pain,
You comforted me.

All my striving, all my
rash enthusiasms, You endured
and yet delighted in me.
I have flung myself into the winds
riding belief like a magic carpet.

Sometimes I soared
and sometimes I fell,
but that instant when all seemed possible
was my tailwind
and ever I would choose it.

Now, I do not.
I sit and read.
I write and dream.
I remember.
I anticipate.

People have failed me
and I have failed others
but we tried.
There is nothing I need now
save You.

Prayer without words

Can it be possible
to breathe in love
as a prayer,
as a blessing?

Not sitting determinedly
in silent contemplation
but moving into and through
every moment of life
trailing sacramental incense
with every step?

When I lay my head on my pillow,
it is your breast,
and when I pull the blanket over me,
it is your love that covers me.

The morning sun is Your
sweet greeting
and the cool breeze
Your hand upon my brow.

Awareness and adoration
so pervasive they need no words.
The butterflies and lightning bugs
are my punctuation,
and the trill of the meadowlark
my exclamation.

I find words so tiresome,
so inadequate,
when instead each breath
is a poem and
each exhalation
a psalm.

Easter children

Little girls
in matching dresses and bows,
sisters in white anklets
and lavender frocks.
A clip-on tie too short
on the little boy,
his white dress shirt escaping
the waistband of his freshly ironed pants.
Hair curled
and hair slicked down.
Tight, new shoes clicking loudly
on the tile floor.
Holding grown-up hands
in a sea of knees.
This is Easter
and it makes no sense to the child,
but for the old ones,
the children in their finery
are harbingers of hope,
portraits of promise.
Somewhere between colored Easter eggs
and flowered crosses
is the truth
of resurrection.

Overnight, Spring

Overnight
the world is greening,
tiny leaves poke out their tender tips,
delicate blossoms unfold tentatively
and everywhere, the grass is greening.
The scent of mountain laurel,
the low, steady hum of honeybees in the hedges,
tulips and jonquils bold, tall and audacious—
the heralds of the season.
There the redbud tree,
a fuchsia crown
so regal among the bare limbs
of its neighbors in the grove.
Birds busy building nests
and the cardinal trilling
a song as brilliant as its plumage.
Everywhere and everything
busies itself with new life
and all the world exclaims
"It is spring! It is spring!"
and the promise returns,
the resurrection in process,
joy spreading in the
softly suffused light of dawn.
This is the day we begin again.

Here. Now.

To live full out
with presence.
Here.
Now.
To smell the cow manure
and yet delight in the calf.
To watch the winds ruffle the lake
and believe their ripples are endless.
To hear the chime tones sound in the wind
and know you stand
in the chapel of God.
To hear the birdsong
and know why they sing.
To see the leafy shadows on the lawn
like tatted lace too fine to touch.
This is life.
This is presence.
This is now.

Hello, baby girl

I couldn't sleep last night. This morning, I have been making casseroles, apple muffins, preparing fresh fruit. Packages are wrapped, cards written, camera battery charged. Today, I meet our first grandchild.

All parties concerned waited and prayed a long time for this little girl's arrival, and on June 27, 2012, at 10:28 a.m., she made her appearance, all 7 lbs., 18 inches of her.

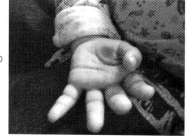

My husband and I have three sons, and so the arrival of a granddaughter was especially thrilling. We venture into a world of femininity I little remember and he never knew; but we are ready! Our son and his wife found out the gender early in the pregnancy, and since then I have become an unabashed Pinkaholic. All my theories about gender messaging and equality flew right out the window, and in came ribbons and bows and laces.

We have seen pictures and movies of this baby girl, but today I will get to hold her, to stare deeply into her already wise eyes and see the image of God, from whom she so recently arrived, looking back at me. I'll get to touch the soft crown of her head and her dark wispy hair and place a kiss upon her brow. I will be able to feel the soft, warm heft of her in the crook of my arm.

This is the full circle of the love that arced between me and a young man 35 years ago when I first slipped my hand into his and felt, as the poet Anne Seton writes, "the world rush in." This is the moment we only imagined when we gave ourselves and our souls to one another wanting to share our love with our own child. This is the moment when I first held our first child—the father of this grandchild—and realized I was holding a mystery I could never unravel or explain. This is Love, and tonight I get to step into that Mystery anew.

I may not sleep tonight either.

Through the birth canal

Life comes unexpectedly,
one night, one coupling,
one determined swimmer,
and Mom is sick every morning
and tired all day
and everybody waits.

I'm here, too,
sort of.
I'm in a good place—
warm waters, good food,
a few weird sounds when
Mom eats tamales
but, hey, I'm good.
I'm not waiting.
I am.

And then things get
a little cramped
and I can't move freely.
I kick and something on the outside
gently pushes my heel back.
Who's out there?

And then, good grief,
a pressure, a clamping
squishes and squeezes me.
What's going on?
And it's happening a lot!
And it hurts a lot!
Mom is really huffing and puffing
and ... I just don't know anymore.
Something's gone really wrong.

Help! Somebody get me outta here!
She's trying to kill me!!!

Then someone's grabbing my head
and pulling on me, and
there is no way
I'm getting through here!
And then I'm freezing—
it's SO cold—
and there's a blinding light.
Is that light?

I don't know what she was
expecting, but I was not expecting this!
And, oh my lord, I'm hanging upside-down
and someone's hitting
my bottom!

Waaaahhhhh!

I want to go back!
Where is my mama,
her smell, her voice?!

Waaaahhhh!

Now I'm wrapped in something
and then handed to someone ...

Mom!!!
You found me!!
Mom, you're not going to believe
what just happened to me!!

Sssh, shhh, shhh, little man.
I've got you.

Ahhhh, well, this may be okay.
I'll give it a try.

Hayes Murray Kabat, Day One.

I am my home

I have traveled far
toward the knowing of myself,
following a dim star
there, just beyond sight,
a glow only
calling me forth.

There were times the darkness
was complete
and then, I followed
only the memory of light.

Around each bend, I thought
I would find it.
This! This is mine to do!
And as I galloped forward
always my foot slipped.

Too often, I looked everywhere
but toward You—
my navigational instruments
no better than yo-yos and
witching sticks.
And so, I led myself astray,
just south of true.

I thought I sought home—
that mythical paradise
always sought by heroes and conquerors,
but also by bums and bunglers.

I sought the welcoming
embrace of the parent—
safety and acceptance and delights—
currency always just out of my reach.

But I am older now,
I see less and know more.
There is no place I long to be,
nothing that calls me forward.
I have travelled all my roads
and they all lead back to me.

I am my home.
I am my new thing.
I am what I sought
and now I am content to stay.
The hounds of hell have
all wandered away
and within me curls
my lap dog—
Yes, we will stay.

There may be those who
are stumbling along
their own paths
and wander into our home.
I will be here
to welcome them,
to love them,
forgive them,
accept them.

I am the answer now
and am living into the
truth of me.

Third-way thinking

Give me two options and I'll choose a third. Some call that opposi-
tional; I prefer to think of it as limitless.

I've never understood "the right answer," which explains my miserable math history. Having only one solution to any challenge is so
confining, so unoriginal, so boring. I suppose because we are failed
creations we need some baselines just to function, but even that is
often problematic for me.

The trouble with either/or is that it leaves out everything
in-between. Dualistic thinking and problem solving means there are
only two answers to any situation, and usually they are either the
way it's always been done or some minuscule variation of the same.
Or, it may just mean one way is dismissed. Why dismiss anything if
you don't have to?

Then there is the question of the creative. I believe God calls us
into continuous co-creativity, and never is that needed moreso in our
world than now. Within creativity is the hope that a better way can
be discovered. Within creativity is unitive thinking, inclusive thinking.
The Great Both/And, the win-win.

Caiaphas, the high priest, gave the people in the courtroom that
day two choices for the future of this Jesus fellow who was creating
such a ruckus: death or life. Two choices that left out the in-between,
the third way.

God had a third way, and in it no one was dismissed or excluded.

Look up!

Rumbling clouds
descend gray and heavy
on a summer sky,
blotting out the crisp blueness
that brushes the horizon.
Rain drops pelt the window
in sudden fury,
each smacking against the pane.
The downpour bounces off
the asphalt parking lot,
streams down car windshields,
obscures sight, heightens senses,
and then stops.
A faucet twisted to off.
Steam rises,
a ray of sun pierces the gray bank
and gleams off drops still puddling.

Look up!
Somewhere
there must be rainbows!

And they followed a star

The seasons of Advent and Christmas are plenteous with metaphors and illustrations to reach us at a different level. Each year, I find I write more during these months than I do at any other time. Every star, every string of tinsel, every makeshift creche seems to have a message. Of course, it does! It is the season of The Message and The Messenger.

I have gathered these into one section. My epiphanies will not be your epiphanies, but my hope is that you will slow down and look, feel, see, know the messages meant for you. They're everywhere!

Waving off Christmas

Over coffee, some friends and I checked in with each other's holiday emotion meter. Holidays come with so many expectations, and all of them are supposed to be joy-filled and magical.

One friend said, "I haven't even thought about it. I'm okay with Jesus, but the rest of it ..." and she waved it off.

That may be the best homily I hear all season.

What have we done to Christmas? I don't mean the mass commercialization and materialism that we've laid upon the season of Advent. Or the sappy songs that get dragged out annually and played *ad nauseum*. Or the fact that the retail kidnapping of Christmas begins the day after Halloween.

I think Advent should be a time as devout as Lent, or at least as we pretend Lent to be. A time of quiet meditation and reflection, of confession and repentance. Most especially a time of "letting go" of anything, material or egotistic, that creates more barriers between ourselves and God. Maybe letting go of the need to "make" everyone's Christmas merry and bright; of cooking the perfect turkey and all its trimmings; of making sure each person has gaily wrapped presents under the tree; of all the doing that keeps us from giving Jesus a single thought.

I'm with my friend: I'm good—really good—with Jesus, and I really wish I had the Christmas balls to wave all the rest of it off.

Light, lighter, lightest

Today, I took down Christmas. Down came the garland and the stockings, the angel tree-topper, the wreath on the door. Down came the cards, the glittery stars and the frolicking snowmen. Down came the hand-painted china figurines of the nativity story, the rough-hewn stable, the blue velvet cloth upon which I place them.

I swept up pine needles and stray ribbons and specks of glitter. Dust bunnies that had hidden beneath gaily wrapped packages now scurried before my broom in search of new cover.

I corralled the last gift bag, tissue paper and gift tag and shut them tightly in their plastic storage box.

Advent is a time of waiting for the Light of God's Son to enter into the darkness of the world and overcome the darkness. We light our Christmas trees, our shrubs and rooftops all as a way to emulate the bright light of the Star in the sky and also to celebrate Jesus as Light.

Lightly also can describe how one carries something. Our troubles can seem heavy and burdensome. Our fears become weighty, indeed, and often we feel weighed down by our insecurities, the economy, global issues—by everything really.

As I untangle the strings of Christmas lights from the tree, I wonder if I can be a daughter of light in this new year, but also a trusting daughter who holds things much more lightly. I will not cling to these old lies I tell myself about who I am; I will hold them lightly. I will not worry about financial misfortunes; I will hold them lightly. I will not grasp at relationships as a way to convince myself I'm worthy of love; I will hold that lightly.

Being light and carrying things lightly is always a tangle. We have to test one bulb at a time and see where the circuit has broken.

Hoarding knickknacks

Putting Christmas away for another year becomes impetus for me to reorganize, consolidate and reduce. I start in the house but that inevitably leads to the garage, which harbors everything except vehicles. It is a rite of purification for me, shamed as I always am by how much "stuff" we possess.

A new year is always a good time to strip away some of this excess. It is a good time for a fresh beginning in my commitment to live more simply and with much less.

Weeding out extra clothes, knickknacks, books, picture frames and plastic cups is easy for me. There are not that many material things I have an emotional attachment to—and they're not in the garage anyway. But when I turn this exercise into one of spiritual mindfulness, I am often appalled at what I hoard in my spirit.

For instance, how stingy am I in freely giving out forgiveness? Or do I stash what little I may possess fearing I will not be able to replenish it? Fearing there will be a bad return on my investment? Worse yet, do I withhold forgiveness until you offer me some first? The same is true of compassion, mercy, grace. I'm not going to give away all that I may possess of these traits (minuscule as that may be) without some assurance I'll get something back—like your undying gratitude, your admiration, your diminishment.

And the hardest emotion of all to freely distribute may be love. Truly loving someone, even the ones you really, really don't like, is akin to emotional nudity. You're exposed and vulnerable and there is no guarantee the love will be returned, or even acknowledged. It is giving someone else complete power over your heart. Oh, I can hold onto my ability to love pretty tightly. I'm not going to squander love, right? Been there, done that and got whomped for it.

Oh yes, I'm glad to let go of that tacky goose cookie jar from the '70s. I just wish I could rid myself as easily of all stinginess of the spirit—the fear, distrust, anger and pain that become the locks to my storehouse.

Giving and receiving

We have just finished a season of giving and receiving gifts, and I realize (anew) that I am often better at giving than I am at receiving. In many ways, this is a good thing: the thought that goes into selecting a gift that is "perfect" for a person, the delight the recipient expresses upon opening the gift, gratitude in knowing someone so well that you can choose the right thing.

It's harder for me to receive gifts, though. I think that may be true for many of us. Is it because we don't like the focus to be on us? That we think we don't deserve such nice things? Is it concern that someone "wasted" so much money on us? That we don't need anything else? If you're into dime-store-variety psychology, you might think there is a tragic self-esteem issue at work here.

I think most Christians have this issue. We love to give—of ourselves, our talents, our tithes. We give casseroles, prayer shawls, and lap blankets. Giving is good. We should give all that we can. We give and give. We give without thinking.

But I don't think we are very well-instructed in receiving, and the gift we have the hardest time receiving is the one represented in the birth of Jesus—the gift of God's love, freedom, redemption and salvation.

"Oh, it's too much," we say. "I don't deserve such a gift!" we exclaim. "Surely that isn't meant for me as well," we defer.

We know about this gift, we sing songs of thanksgiving for its arrival, we bow before the Giver, we even tell others about this gift. But, I still contend, very few of us have really received this gift. We have not dived deeply into it, swam in it, breathed it in all the way to our toes and back. We have not felt it flow through us as the Living Water it is, or experienced it lift and sustain us.

Because once we have received it, everything else falls away. It isn't about deserving it or earning it or being worthy of it. We aren't. We can't be. That's why it is pure gift. And that's why it really isn't ours until we can accept it, fully.

Lord, help me stop giving long enough to receive your love, your joy, your peace. Then, all that I am and do will be gift to others.

The pregnant pause

Many of us are observing Advent in the coming weeks. There are so many ways for us to describe what it meant to the world for Jesus to enter into it as a helpless infant—savior, king, redeemer, teacher. Or what his presence represents—love, forgiveness, mercy, grace, patience.

We have a 3-month-old grandson and we were so blessed this past Thanksgiving weekend to have him and his parents with us! There is no denying, however, that an infant in your life changes everything. It changes your sleep pattern, your focus, your priorities, your daily schedule, and your financial situation. And it most certainly changes how you think about things.

Is that any different from what Jesus's presence in our world asks of us? He came into all of our homes and hearts and with the piercing wail that only an infant can emit said, "Here I am! Wake up! Pay attention to me!" and like an infant his cry said, "I need you!"

Remember back to the days and nights of your firstborn. It wasn't easy, it was often frustrating, there were so many fears and so much lack of self-confidence. You had so much responsibility and you felt it so keenly. But there also was indescribable joy, sweet moments of looking into the eyes of divinity as they stare trustingly up at you, a heart connection that comes when a miracle is sowed, nurtured and birthed.

The world is expecting a new baby! The holy sonogram assures us it's a boy! Let's clean out that spare bedroom in our mind of its clutter and chaos, and prepare a place for him.

We're having a Son!

The agony of Advent

Advent is defined by expectation; we wait expectantly for the birth of the Savior. We wait expectantly with hope and joy.

These weeks before the remembering of the holy birth are filled with other expectations, as well. Of the perfect gift, of joyous family gatherings, of happy songs and red dresses and sparkly joy. As Clark Griswold says in the movie "Christmas Vacation," "the hap-hap-happiest Christmas" ever.

Both the religious and the secular ride these waves of expectation—to be saved, liberated, made whole, find meaning—whether by Jesus's transcendent love or by the Tiffany necklace we covet. And whether we are religious or not, the expectation within us often is reduced to the same shallow wish.

When the wrapping paper and ribbon are gathered in the trash bag and the baby Jesus figurine stuffed back in a box, what do we actually have? How have we changed?

Not every person can manufacture joy and glad tidings in preparation for Christmas. Many are dealing with mental illness, depression, a reversal in life circumstances, losses of many kind, chronic pain or illness—and no amount of glittering lights or shiny tinsel can disguise this very real suffering.

But there is also a foreshadowing at Christmas that should cause us solemn pause. The gifts the magi brought included spices used for embalming. And so, in the manger that night was born both new life and everlasting life—for those who would believe and live into that belief. Yet we continue to reduce the hard teaching of the gospel into platitudes and analgesics, as though Jesus's birth and death and resurrection are only about comforting and excusing us.

In this season of Advent I want to yell up to God, "Don't do it! Don't send your Son! We won't recognize him or believe him and we certainly won't do as he asks us to do. Don't send this infant into the world because we absolutely will kill him. Save him! He doesn't deserve this!"

We are not a teachable people.

We have trivialized the revolutionary significance of Emmanuel—God with us—in the same way we have his death and resurrection at Easter. Candy canes and jelly beans do not transform us.

I mourn as I wait for the Christ child because I have found "expectation" to be profoundly untrustworthy. An event that should fell us to our knees in awe and humility instead has become an imperative to "go, go, go, shop, shop, shop."

Shouldn't the one who gave up everything and came to earth to be one of us get more respect? Shouldn't this sacrifice "to become nothing" for our sake change us? Change how we live, how we love?

If we have the nerve to pray "Come, Lord Jesus," then we better be prepared—as the wise men discovered—to go home another way. Our path and our destination have changed.

A Christmas rainbow

Christmas is a season of symbols: Santa and reindeer, mistletoe and fir trees. There are two other symbols I think of at Christmas: a broken heart and dancing rainbows.

It began six years ago when our family traveled to Nebraska for what would be our last Christmas with both my in-laws, whom everyone called ViVi and Cuzzy. I can still see their smiles and excited waves when they saw our old station wagon pull up to their home.

It was a fun-filled, boisterous few days, with all of the extended family gathered together. The grandchildren crawled into ViVi's lap for bedtime stories, ran to her for fresh-baked gingerbread boys and giggled as she sang funny songs.

I had looked a long time for a Christmas present for ViVi that year. I wanted to give her something that would symbolize what she meant to us. She always put the needs of her husband and children first. She was the heart of her family.

I finally found what I was searching for—a beautiful, lacy glass heart to hang in the window. ViVi so enjoyed prisms and stained glass hangings that caught the sun's rays. She filled her kitchen with dancing rainbows.

ViVi's face lit up when she unwrapped the glass heart. She gave me a hug and immediately put it in her bedroom window. During the rest of our stay, I often saw her slip back into the bedroom to admire the fragile heart.

Too soon it was time for us to leave. As she always did when we left, ViVi stood on the front stoop and waved goodbye, trying to hide her tears.

The months passed quickly after we returned home. Then suddenly, our lives were punctuated by the first of many frightening phone calls. ViVi was in the hospital. She was having trouble with her heart. She would need a triple bypass.

Then, too quickly for us to grasp, she was gone, unable to survive the operation.

Stunned, my husband and his siblings gathered once again in .Nebraska. Circumstances prevented the children and I from going. On a cold, misty spring day, they said goodbye to ViVi. Hundreds of miles away, I sat staring numbly out the window.

A month later, we all went to Nebraska to spend time with Cuzzy. ViVi's smiling face was not there to greet us this time. Walking into their home, the reality of her loss hit me full force.

Until that visit, I had managed to deny ViVi's death. Now there was no escaping it. Cuzzy wanted me to pack her clothes and costume jewelry. It was a heart-breaking task, and I soon had to step away from it to collect my thoughts. I went to the window and pulled open the drapes. As sunshine filled the room, I saw something glitter.

At first, I didn't realize what it was. When I did, the tears that had threatened so many times finally spilled over. There on the windowsill were the shattered pieces of the glass heart I had given ViVi for Christmas. Its suction cup had loosened and the heart had broken.

Carefully, I brushed the pieces into my hand. The sun shone through the fragments and sent dancing rays of color into the room.

I stood there for a long time that day. I let the tears fall and I let my heart grieve. It was an ending, but also a beginning. The heart of this family had not been broken beyond repair, as had the glass heart in my hand. The light of ViVi's love could still cast rainbows into our lives.

Every Christmas Day since, I have slipped away from the piles of toys and the laughing children. I find a quiet place to sit and think about ViVi and broken hearts. And, once again, I look for the dancing rainbows in my world.

Viola Anna Kabat
May 24, 1988

Candle of Hope

I am a person prone to despair. I do not like this about myself. I especially felt contrite last night at worship when the first Advent candle—Hope—was lit.

You really can't call yourself a follower of Christ and not live in hope. There is no such thing as a hopeless Christian. We profess that our hope is in the Resurrected Christ.

You see my dilemma.

There is so much wrong and evil and inexplicable in our world that with every new headline, I ask God, "How long? How long?"

When babies are born with rare brain malformations, when addicted mothers get clean and try so hard but then relapse, when 3-year-olds use the f-bomb as easily as they use their fists, I am prone to despair. And those are incidents just in my own circles.

I relate more to the author of Ecclesiastes, it seems, than to the Good News.

It's easy in this season leading up to the remembrance of Jesus's birth to confuse "wish" and "hope." Wish is Santa Claus but hope is Jesus, as our pastor said last night. Children have a hard time waiting for Christmas morning. As Christian adults, we must live by Romans 8:25: *"But if we hope for what we do not yet have, we wait for it patiently."*

So, I light my Hope candle at home. This is not the world I want, nor is it the one its Creator wanted. In these weeks, it is a world covered over in glitter and tinsel while the world of Mary and Joseph was one of straw and manure.

Look into the night sky past the multicolored lights along the eaves and search for the star. Wait for it. Patiently wait for the light. It is our beacon of hope.

Have we lost Christmas?

There is a point after Christmas when I arise from bed and know, like the timer buzzing on the oven, that I need to get Christmas decorations down and packed away. Today was that day. As I was working, I thought about something our pastor says: "As Christians, we have surrendered the meaning of the birth of Jesus to our culture. It is a battle we've lost."

As I rolled sparkly tinsel and bubble-wrapped delicate ornaments, I wrestled with that thought. Does Christmas still have meaning for us as followers of Christ? If so, what is it?

I remember the things I told our children as they grew: We give presents because the Wise Men brought gifts to the baby Jesus; Santa is not real but an infant savior is; be grateful even if you don't like what you got. We bumbled our way through a Ho-Ho-Holy celebration, and I'm not sure any of the true meaning of the occasion took hold or made sense.

That's a reflection on our parenting abilities, I suppose. Yet, with the kids grown and gone, do I have any better understanding of this holiday? Do you?

The gifts the wise men brought were premonitions of the baby's death 30 years hence. A helpless infant born to save his people still seems less plausible to most of us than a jolly fat man who lives at the North Pole. And we rotely recite the Lord's Prayer every week without any thought of the gift we really received, much less gratitude for it.

Putting away Christmas makes me sad. Oh, I'm well tired of the glitter and sparkle, but the emptiness of the room after the tree comes down reflects the spiritual emptiness I feel in our world.

We didn't get the gift we wanted, the one that was promised. We got a baby. And nothing changed. The angels left, the star moved on, and the wise men went home.

What would be a better way to remember Christmas? How could we make Jesus's presence among us palpable every day? How would that change us?

The quiet Christmas

When I was director of Christian education at a small Presbyterian church for a few years, I learned many things. I learned where the upstairs mop bucket was. I learned to get to church early when there had been rain the night before so I could mop up the 5th grade Sunday School room floor where the roof leaked. I learned where the toilet paper and the plunger were kept. I learned how to launder and iron the altar cloths and the Fellowship Hall table linens.

And I learned what to do when the curious hands of a 6-year-old accidentally beheads the wooden figure of one of the three kings of the Christmas pageant. Chewing gum will hold together body and head and the histrionics of a child so that the procession may occur.

I think about that decapitated wise man a lot during the Christmas season, and its conclusion on Epiphany Sunday. The scripture tells us that these astrologers from the Far East had seen a great light in the night sky and had traveled far to find it. Unlike most men in generations since, they stopped to ask directions, but unfortunately stopped in at Herod's place.

"Where is the new king whose coming is announced in the night sky?" they asked Herod, the sitting king. Unwittingly their question unleashed political chaos and territorial machinations in their wake as they moved on through the desert, their gifts in hand.

Some speculate it was two to three years after the infant's birth before the magi found their way to the house of Mary, Joseph and the young Jesus. A long, arduous, unsure journey guided only by a light and their steadfast belief. And when they finally arrived, they bowed down to worship the toddler and offer him their gifts of gold, incense and myrrh.

It doesn't seem impossible, or even preposterous, to me that a wise man on such a journey might lose his head. I have sought the infant Jesus most of my adult life. I have traveled across barren terrain and through dark nights, believing (or wanting to believe) a light was guiding me. Being female, I stopped many times along the way to ask directions—of pastors, spiritual guides, noted theologians, my neighbor across the backyard fence, the child mesmerized by a butterfly. "Have you seen the light?" "Do you know the way?" "Am

I heading in the right direction?" And more often than I care to admit, I lost my head on this journey—sometimes because it swelled too big with arrogance and sometimes because it shriveled with insignificance and unworthiness.

Such a long, hard journey fraught with error, danger, uncertainty. I wearied and faltered. At times, I set up my tent and just stopped, withdrawn and discouraged. At other times, I stumbled upon an oasis and joined with other maidens to dance around the well and pull from its depths.

When I finally stood at the threshold of my Savior's home, prepared to kneel before him, I realized I was in a familiar place, a site I knew, if only faintly. Why, this hearth was my own! the Christ child lay within me, in the space somewhere between my spirit and soul that spreads like late spring's greenest pastures, waiting to welcome me ... Home. Home, that mysterious place where you see yourself reflected in God's mirror, as Richard Rohr writes, and you recognize yourself for the first time.

And so I lay myself before the new King, for I am the gift.

"It's perfect," I hear Mary say. "Exactly what he has been longing for!"

Lifetime of love reflected in a kiss

I watched a love story the other night. It wasn't on television or at the movie theater. But it was the most moving love story I've ever seen. And though it lasted but a moment, the memory of it will be with me forever.

It began nearly 53 years ago when a young woman named Asa Lee Walters applied for a job at Citizens Investment Trust in Texarkana. The manager who took her application that day was a handsome young fellow named W. O. (Mac) McDonald. They dated, fell in love and, seven months later, married.

Shortly thereafter, Mac was called into the Air Force after Pearl Harbor and served for three years. Upon his release, CIT transferred the McDonalds to Waco.

They reared a son and a daughter, were active in their church and enjoyed the arrival over the years of five grandchildren. Their lives had been full until a couple of years ago when Mac's health began to fail.

I met Mrs. McDonald a few nights ago as several of us gathered to sing Christmas carols for hospitalized and homebound members of our church. I couldn't help but notice her. Her ready smile and easy laugh would make her stand out in any group.

I was especially surprised, then, to learn our first stop was to visit Mrs. McDonald's husband at the Veterans Administration Medical Center. He suffers from a congestive heart failure and Parkinson's disease, which makes speech nearly impossible for him. He also has an eye condition that has robbed him of his sight, except for slight peripheral vision. It is hard for him to see faces.

By the time we entered Mac's room, our group had quieted, sobered by the suffering we saw around us. Mac was awake, but he didn't seem to recognize his wife, who bent to kiss his cheek and take his hand.

We did our best, singing "Silent Night" and "Joy to the World," We didn't feel very joyful, though. Some of us fought back tears. Our songs seemed small comfort to offer.

As we sang, Mrs. McDonald leaned over her husband's bed and looked lovingly into his unseeing eyes. Perhaps she saw reflected in them the joys of Christmases past, of their children playing on his lap, of tender moments they had shared.

Our singing ended and Mrs. McDonald bent nearer to her husband, smiling, to say a few words before she turned to leave. He was unable to respond.

Taking our cue, we started for the door. But I looked back and saw Mac, who had been still throughout our visit, trying to move.

He seemed to understand his wife was leaving. With great difficulty, he turned his head and reached out his hand toward her.

For a moment I was afraid she wouldn't notice his movements. She seemed connected to him by some invisible thread, though, because just then she looked back. Seeing his outstretched hand, she instantly returned to his side and grasped it, bending near to give him another kiss.

When she rejoined us, her smile was still there and her spirit was dampened only by the tears on her cheeks.

The clasped hands and the shared kiss had taken only a moment, yet the love of which it spoke is part of a timeless story. A story as ancient as creation and as new as tomorrow's sunrise, when once again Mrs. McDonald will return to her husband's side.

It is a love story for all time.

A final gift

As a friend and member of her church, I sat vigil with her for several hours Friday night. Her mother, her three adult children, her sister, her former husband—they moved softly in and out of the dimly lit room, taking turns at her bedside. She was mostly incoherent from the morphine she was receiving every 30 minutes; she needed it every 10 minutes, and still it barely dulled her intense pain.

She cried out, she begged us to do something, she said she couldn't stand it any longer. We had already asked the nurses to give her more, something else, anything. So all we had to offer her was our presence, our touch, whispered words in her ear: "We're here. You're safe. We love you." And our prayers. "Please, God, take her home. Please."

Like many families, this one was large and often dysfunctional. There had been years of estrangements, hard words, disappointments, bad choices followed by more bad choices. Just this side of death, none of that matters.

Between the rails of a hospital bed, a mother's hand encircled her dying daughter's hand. "I'm here, baby. I'm here." And we all clung to the only thing we know that is strong enough to carry us to the edge of death: love. We are born into love and we die into love, and all the journey between, imperfect and difficult as it can be, is a searching after that love.

I walked away in the early morning hours, but others remained and saw her dying through to the next day. Now she was home, now she was free, now her pain was over. Ours, on the other hand, was just beginning.

We're the ones left to ask ourselves why we didn't try harder, love more, forgive more, resent less. I now know for a fact—a fact as cold and unyielding as the deepest pain—that no other effort in life is more important.

Conclusion

The first time I wrote in response to a mass shooting, it was in reference to the Columbine High School tragedy in 1999. Never could I have dreamed that so many more senseless acts of violence involving military-style weapons would ensue. As I finish this compilation, it is summer 2019. In one week recently, America experienced four mass shootings. Four in one week. While I had worked with this book for a couple of years, it was not until that horrific week that I was motivated to finish it. It became very clear to me that this was what I could do in the face of so much anger and hatred in our country. This book was mine to do. I hope a few of the words here encourage, calm, enlighten, comfort you.

I close this collection with an essay I wrote that was printed in our local newspaper. I believe the subject of it is the right role model and encouragment for the days ahead.

Mr. Rogers, are you home?

When all the world seems to be imploding, I don't know what is mine to do. I turn my heart to this and then to that and the next day there is a new insult to humanity and nature. I dizzy myself with the actions around me that I find abhorrent, immoral, and un-American. Where do I focus when there no longer is a greater vision? I had given up asking "How much worse can it get?" as I did in the early days. Now I know there is no limit to how bad it can get. It's a freefall of narcissism that builds like a snowball racing downhill, growing ever bigger as it flings protests aside so effortlessly.

Maybe the better metaphor is the lava continuously spewing from Hawaii's Kilauea Volcano (May 2018). It erupts at will sending lava throughout cities and destroying everything in its path. Just as we think the flow may be abating, a new eruption occurs—and once again we are engulfed in smoke and chaos.

Someone asked me recently what I'm doing in retirement. I told them I've begun a new vocation: social activist. But the number of social injustices raining down on us is catastrophic. We are caught in a mudslide of destruction because our firm foundations of ethics and truth are so severely eroded. We are caught in the natural catastrophes we see every night in the news. They are our new reality. Is this Armageddon?

A friend asked me the other day if I could write an editorial about what's going on in the world. I looked at him bleakly and said, "I wouldn't know where to begin."

Get out and vote—Yes! Protest against injustice—Yes! Write your congresspersons—Yes! Pray, pray and pray—Yes! Yet each can seem like the spotty drops of moisture that fall into the heat of a Texas summer day—a cruel promise of rain that doesn't materialize.

I want to grow 50 feet tall and stomp around the earth shouting, "Stop it! You are all behaving badly! No more! Can't you see you're destroying each other?"

In that mindset, then, I went to see the 2018 documentary film on Fred Rogers titled "Won't You Be My Neighbor?" I admit, I longed to hear his gentle voice, to witness his sincerity and his unconditional love. I was absolutely undone by his kindness and determination to treat each child with respect. "I love you just the way you are."

I wept. I learned later from many friends that they wept, too. After the hate-filled rhetoric from Washington, D.C., and across the nation, it was cathartic to be bathed in gentleness and acceptance.

Our nation has become a fiery feud between the Hatfields and McCoys. We used to worry about bipartisanship across the aisle, and now we worry about it across the country. I still believe, though, that most of us in the extended families just want to sit under the oak tree, drink lemonade, and remember the family stories that initially shaped us.

Perhaps it will take our tears to put out the lava flow. If that is so, cry. Cry for all that we took for granted, for all that we let slip away. I'll hold you while you cry and you hold me while I cry. I only know this. We each long to be visible, valued and appreciated. We each long to be loved just the way we are.

Some people mocked Fred Rogers for what they saw as his simplistic message of love, yet there is nothing harder in the world to do than to love your neighbor. It's been 50 years since Mr. Rogers said it, millennia since Jesus said it, and we still haven't done it. We have to try again.

Vicki Marsh Kabat enjoys her retirement after a career in journalism, marketing and publications. She is the founding editor of the award-winning *Baylor Magazine,* an alumni publication for Baylor University. Her first book, *MomSense: For Clueless Parents Everywhere,* is a humorous look at raising three sons with her husband, Bruce. She also is the author and illustrator of a children's book titled *Will You Still Love Me?,* available on Amazon.com.

Kabat and her husband live in Waco, Texas. She is available to lead contemplative prayer and silent retreats. She also is a spiritual director. She can be contacted through her website or email address:

www.kabatkind.com
Vkabat@gmail.com

Printed in the United States
By Bookmasters